POTA

A collection of delicio

Contents

Introduction   3

Breakfast   7

Soups & Snacks   13

Salads   23

Lunch   31

Main Meals   41

Side Dishes   61

Cakes & Bakes   85

Index   91

Text by Sara Porter

Originally published in 2009 by L&K Designs. This edition published for Myriad Books Limited in 2010.
© L&K Designs 2009
PRINTED IN CHINA

Publishers Disclaimer

The recipes contained in this book are passed on in good faith but the publisher cannot be held responsible for any adverse results. Please be aware that certain recipes may contain nuts.

Potatoes

Boasting an impressive history, the potato has long been a staple food for many cultures and nationalities. Potatoes come in a wide range of tastes, colours and textures, in old and new varieties and are cultivated in local and distant lands.

Fortunately, we are no longer limited to uniform varieties of potatoes in our supermarkets and farm shops, we've been opened up to a new world of mouth-watering national and international varieties, offering a diverse range of tastes, textures and flavours.

Potatoes are a great source of nutrition, being low in fat and calories and high in vitamin C, B6 and fibre. They also boast an enviable versatility being served in simple, traditional, stylish, elegant and vibrant dishes... and not forgetting good old fashioned favourites... such as mash, chips, jackets, roasties, etc...

Economically friendly and abundantly plentiful; potatoes are perfect for making affordable and nutritious meals, offering satisfying and delicious choices for the whole family. We've included a great range of choices including classic gratins, deliciously different baked potato and creamy mash recipes, warming soups, spicy wedges, mouth-watering roasts, yummy salads, hearty pies, substantial bakes, curries and much, much more... there's even a potato pizza!

Written in easy step-by-step instructions and offering basic potato classics through to more adventurous and exotic meal ideas, this book offers over 90 potato-based recipes from soups, lunches and light dishes, salads, side dishes and accompaniments, to main meals and even some sweet options!

Choosing Potatoes

Potatoes come in a variety of different shapes, sizes, textures and colours - brown, purple, red, white or golden... there are a plethora of different varieties to choose from.

Although there are no hard and fast rules as to what type of potatoes you should be using when cooking, it's true that certain types of potato are better suited to particular types of cooking.

The list below provides a guide to general potato types and their recommended uses.

Cooking Purpose	Type of Potato
Baking	Marfona, Estima, Cara, Golden Wonder, Vivaldi, Russett, Idaho
Chips	Maris Piper, Estima, King Edward, Golden Wonder, Sante, Pentland Dell, Desiree
Mashing	Pentland Dell, King Edward, Pentland Squire, Vivaldi
Roasting	Desiree, Cara, Wilja, Pentland Dell
Salad	Jersey Royal, Ratte, Charlotte, Pink Fir Apple, Vales Emerald
Boiling	Vivaldi, Yukon Gold, Cara, Estima, Saxon, Nadine, Pink Fir Apple
All-Rounders (except for salads & steaming)	Maris Piper, King Edward, Desiree, Romano

Storing Potatoes
Cool and dark
Store in a cool, dark, dry place – with lots of ventilation. The perfect temperature is between 7C and 10C.

No direct sun
Do not expose potatoes to direct sunlight as this can cause them to turn green.

No polythene bags
Never store in polythene bags or plastic bags, as this increases condensation and creates perfect conditions for the growth of mould.

Avoid warmth
Avoid storing potatoes in a pantry or warm cupboard, as this can lead to dehydration and premature sprouting.

Refrigerators
Do not store in refrigerators under 7C, as this causes the potatoes to develop a sweet taste.

Separate

Keep separate from strong smelling foods.

Onions

Never store potatoes with onions as they both omit gases which spoil each other.

Blemishes

Blemished and green patches on skins should be removed, as these contain toxins.

Check regularly

Check stored potatoes regularly. If there are sprouted, soft or shrivelled potatoes in the batch, remove the offending potatoes immediately and discard.

Storage time

Sweet potatoes and new potatoes should be stored for no longer than 1 week. Old potatoes can be stored for longer periods, for 4-6 weeks.

Hash Browns (Serves 4)

Ingredients

500g/1.1lbs peeled & cooked potatoes (diced)
1 medium onion (finely chopped)
4 tbsps vegetable oil
salt & black pepper (to season)

Directions

1. Heat the oil in a large frying pan and add the potatoes, forming a single layer of potato chunks. Sprinkle the onion over the top and season with salt and black pepper.

2. Cook over a medium heat, until golden brown underneath, regularly pressing the potatoes down with a spatula or the back of a wooden spoon.

3. Once browned underneath, cut the hash into quarters and turn each over using a fish slice. Cook again, until golden brown and heated through.

4. Serve immediately.

Mexican Potatoes (Serves 4)
Ingredients
3 medium potatoes (peeling is optional)

1 small onion (diced)

1 red pepper (diced)

Jalapeno pepper (finely diced) (optional)

3 tsps salsa

salt and pepper to taste

Directions
1. Par-boil the potatoes for about 15 to 20 minutes.

2. Slice the potatoes in about 1 inch chuncks. Heat 2 tablespoons of oil in a skillet over medium high heat and add all the ingredients. Semi brown your potatoes on both sides, 5 or 6 minutes should do it. Serve with eggs or in a tortilla wrap.

Potato, Cheese & Bacon Omelette (Serves 3-4)
Ingredients
325g/11oz new potatoes (scrubbed & diced)

6 rashers of back bacon (chopped)

80g/3oz Cheddar cheese (grated)

4 large eggs (beaten)

1 tbsp milk

salt & black pepper (to season)

Directions
1. Cook the new potatoes for 12-15 minutes, until tender. Drain and set to one side.

2. Heat the oil in frying pan, add the bacon and cook for 4-5 minutes. Add the diced potatoes and cook for 1-2 minutes.

3. Place the eggs in a bowl and add the milk and 40g of the cheese. Season with salt and black pepper and beat together. Add the mixture to the frying pan and cook over a medium heat for 3-4 minutes, until partially set.

4. Whilst the omelette is cooking, preheat the grill to a medium heat.

5. Sprinkle the remaining cheese over the top of the omelette and cook for further minute. Remove from the heat and place the pan under the grill. Cook until the omelette is set and lightly golden on top.

Serve immediately.

Potato, Chorizo & Egg Brunch (Serves 4)
Ingredients
525g/1lb 3oz salad potatoes (scrubbed & thickly sliced)
250g/9oz chorizo sausage (skinned & sliced)
4 eggs
bunch of spring onions (sliced)
1 1/2 tbsps olive oil

Directions
1. Cook the potatoes for 4-5 minutes. Drain, return to the pan and stir in the olive oil.

2. Heat a frying pan and add the potatoes. Cook for 7-8 minutes, until golden brown.

3. Heat a large, separate frying pan and add the chorizo sausage and spring onions. Cook for 3-4 minutes. Add the potatoes and toss all the ingredients together.

4. Whilst the sausage and spring onions are frying, poach the eggs in boiling water.

5. Transfer the potato mixture to 4 individual serving dishes and top each with a poached egg.

Potato Pancake

Ingredients

3-4 tbsps olive oil

5 large russet potatoes

12 slices bacon, cooked and crumbled

1 cup/9 oz grated cheese

coarse salt to taste

ground pepper to taste

small bunch chives, cleaned and snipped

Directions

1. Preheat oven to 220C/425F/Gas mark 7.

2. Oil a ceramic quiche dish with a teaspoon of the olive oil.

3. Grate the potatoes into a bowl, working as quickly as possible to prevent them from turning brown. (You can put the grated potatoes in a bowl of cold water while grating the rest, but dry really well before using.)

4. Transfer half of the shredded potatoes to the prepared dish. Sprinkle with some of the coarse salt, a few grindings of pepper, a few drizzles of olive oil, half the bacon and half of the cheese. Put the remaining potatoes in dish and repeat the salt, pepper, olive oil, bacon and cheese.

5. Roast until potatoes are dark brown and crisp on top yet soft inside, 50-55 minutes. If the potatoes begin to brown too quickly, reduce the oven temperature down to 180C/350F/Gas mark 4.

6. Remove from oven and let rest for 5-10 minutes, sprinkle with chives, then cut into wedges. Serve immediately.

Potato Scones (Makes 12)

Ingredients

450g/1lb floury potatoes (peeled & cut into chunks)
100g/2/3 cup self-raising flour
50g/2oz butter
1/2 tsp salt
1 tbsp butter
chopped chives

Directions

1. Boil the potatoes for 15-20 minutes, until soft. Drain thoroughly and mash. Add the 50g of butter and salt and mash again.

2. Gradually add the flour, continuing to mash. The mixture should become thick and stiff.

3. Turn out onto a clean, floured surface and knead lightly. Using a rolling pin, roll out to a thickness of 1/2 inch. Cut with a scone shape-cutter, or cut into triangles.

4. Heat the remaining butter in a griddle and cook for 4-5 minutes on each side, until golden. Serve hot.

Sausage Hash

Ingredients

2 packages of sausage meat (approx 500g/1.1lbs)
2 cups/300g potatoes chopped and boiled
1 small onion finely chopped
salt and pepper freshly ground
4 tbsps butter
5 tbsps heavy cream

Directions

1. Cut the sausage meat into small pieces. In a large frying pan over medium-low heat, cook the sausage, stirring and separating until the sausage is browned (about 10 minutes). Using a slotted spoon, transfer the sausage to a bowl. Discard the fat in the pan.

2. Add potatoes and onion to the sausage and mix well. Add salt and pepper to taste.

3. Melt the butter in a frying pan. Spread the sausage mixture over the bottom and press down with a spatula. Fry over medium-low heat for 15-20 minutes.

4. Use the spatula to have a look at the underside. If it is nicely browned, turn the hash over. Slide it out on a dinner plate and invert the plate over the skillet.

5. Pour cream evenly over the meat and cook for another 15 to 20 minutes until the second side is nicely brown.

Chilled Potato Soup (Serves 6)

Ingredients

650g/1 1/2lbs potatoes (peeled & diced)
250ml/1 cup soured cream
3 avocados (peeled & flesh removed)
1 large onion (chopped)
1 1/2 litres/6 cups of vegetable stock
3/4 tsp chilli flakes
1 1/2 tbsps vegetable oil
chopped coriander (to garnish)
salt & black pepper (to season)

Directions

1. Place the avocado flesh in a bowl, cover and set to one side.

2. Heat the oil in a saucepan, over a medium heat and add the onion. Cook for 4-5 minutes, until tender. Add the chilli flakes and cook for 2-3 minutes.

3. Add the diced potatoes and vegetable stock. Bring to the boil. Reduce the heat, cover and simmer for 12-15 minutes, until tender.

4. Remove from the heat and leave to cool a little. Transfer to a food processor (you may need to do this in batches), and blend until smooth. Leave to cool.

5. Add the avocado and soured cream to the mixture and blend again. Season with salt and black pepper, according to taste. Leave until completely cooled, before covering and placing the refrigerator to chill.

6. Serve cold, with a garnish of chopped coriander.

Cream of Potato Soup (Serves 4)
Ingredients
450g/1lb potatoes (peeled & diced)
2 sticks of celery (sliced)
1 onion (thinly sliced)
300ml/1 1/4 cups milk
3 tbsps double cream
450ml/2 cups water
25g/1oz butter
2 tbsps fresh parsley (chopped)
salt & black pepper (to season)

Directions
1. Heat the butter in a large saucepan and add the onion, potatoes and celery. Cook over a gentle heat for 8-10 minutes – do not brown.

2. Add the water and season with salt and black pepper, according to taste. Bring to the boil, cover and reduce the heat then simmer for 25 minutes. Remove from the heat and leave to cool a little.

3. Transfer the soup to a food processor and process until smooth (you may need to do this in a couple of batches).

4. Return to the saucepan and add the milk. Bring to the boil, stirring continuously. Reduce the heat and simmer for 5 minutes.

5. Transfer to individual serving bowls and swirl with a little cream. Garnish with chopped parsley and serve.

Crispy Potato Skins & Tex Mex Dips (Serves 12)
Ingredients
12 large jacket potatoes
150g/1 1/2 cups of Cheddar cheese (grated)
olive oil cooking spray (or olive oil)
2 tubs of mild salsa
2 tubs of soured cream with chives
2 tubs of guacamole

Directions

1. Preheat the oven to 180C/350F/Gas mark 4. Line 2 baking trays with non-stick baking paper.

2. Place the jacket potatoes in the oven and bake for 1 to 1 1/2 hours, until cooked. Remove from the oven and leave to cool a little for 10-15 minutes.

3. Cut the potatoes in half lengthways, and spoon out the potato leaving about 5mm of potato flesh inside. With a sharp knife, slice each piece into 3 pieces, lengthways.

4. Place the potato skins on the baking trays and spray with the cooking oil (or brush with olive oil). Sprinkle over the grated cheese and place in the oven for 20-25 minutes, until gold and crispy.

5. Remove from the oven and leave to cool a little. Serve with the dips!

Moroccan-Style Potato & Chickpea Soup (Serves 4-6)

Ingredients

400g/1 2/3 cups canned chickpeas (drained)
1 onion (finely chopped)
2 carrots (finely diced)
1 celery stick (finely diced)
400g/1 3/4 cups of canned chopped tomatoes
350g/2 cups of new potatoes (finely diced)
1ltr/4 1/2 cups of hot vegetable stock
1 tbsp lemon juice
1 tsp cinnamon
1 tbsp fresh root ginger (grated)
1 tsp turmeric
2 tbsps fresh coriander (chopped)
salt & black pepper (to season)

Directions

To be cooked in a slow cooker at a high temperature.

1. Place the chopped onion and 600ml of the vegetable stock into the slow cooker. Cover and cook for 1 hour.

Moroccan-Style Potato & Chickpea Soup cont/.

2. Place the spices and 2 tbsps of the stock in a bowl and mix together to make a paste. Add to the slow cooker, followed by the remaining stock, celery and carrots. Stir in well and season with salt and black pepper. Cover and cook for 1 hour.

3. Add the potatoes, chopped tomatoes and chickpeas and cook for 4-5 hours.

4. Once cooked, stir in the lemon juice and coriander and serve immediately.

Olive & Caper Potato Cakes (Serves 4)

Ingredients

2 large baking potatoes (peeled & cut into 3/4 inch/2cm pieces)
8 kalamata black olives (finely chopped)
2 tsps jarred capers (drained & finely chopped)
2 large eggs (lightly beaten)
2/3 cup/70g dry bread crumbs
1/2 cup/110ml vegetable oil
lemon wedges

Directions

1. Boil the potatoes for 8-10 minutes, until tender. Drain well and set aside for 5 minutes.

2. Mash the potato and stir in the olives, capers and eggs, mixing them in well. Season with salt and black pepper, according to taste.

3. Place the breadcrumbs on a plate.

4. Separate the mixture into 8 equally-sized pieces and shape into 1/2 inch thick cakes. Coat evenly with breadcrumbs.

5. Heat the vegetable oil in a large frying pan and add the cakes. Cook for 2-3 minutes each side, until golden brown.

6. Serve hot with lemon wedges.

Potato & Pasta Soup (Serves 2)

Ingredients

2 large potatoes (peeled & diced)
1 onion (finely chopped)
225g/1/2lb of macaroni pasta
500g/16oz canned, crushed tomatoes
225ml/1 cup water
1 tbsp olive oil
Parmesan cheese (grated)
salt & black pepper (to season)

Directions

1. Heat the oil in a saucepan and add the onion. Cook for 3-4 minutes, until lightly browned. Add the tomatoes and water and bring to the boil. Reduce the heat and simmer for 35-40 minutes.

2. Meanwhile, cook the potatoes and pasta in a large pan for 10 minutes. Drain the water, leaving in just enough to cover the top of the potatoes and pasta.

3. Stir the onion/tomato mixture into the saucepan with the potatoes and pasta and heat through for a few of minutes. Season with salt and black pepper, according to taste.

4. Remove from the heat and transfer to serving bowls. Serve topped with a little grated Parmesan cheese.

Potato & Smoked Fish Chowder (Serves 4)

Ingredients

2 large potatoes (diced)
450g/1lb smoked haddock (skinned & cut into large chunks)
1 onion (sliced)
1 leek (finely sliced)
1/2 red pepper (finely chopped)
200g/1 1/4 cups canned sweetcorn (drained)
300ml/1 1/3 cups milk
1 bay leaf
2 tbsps fresh parsley (chopped)
50g/2oz butter
275ml/10fl oz water

Directions

1. Place the butter in a large saucepan and melt the butter over a medium heat. Then add the leek, onion and red pepper. Cook for 3-4 minutes, stirring frequently.

2. Stir in the potatoes, coating them well. Reduce the heat, cover and cook for 5-6 minutes, stirring frequently.

3. Add the fish, milk, water, bay leaf and bring to the boil. Reduce the heat again, cover and simmer for 12-15 minutes, until the fish is cooked through.

4. Stir in the sweetcorn and cook for a further 3 minutes. Discard the bay leaf and ladle in to the 4 serving bowls and serve hot. Garnish with chopped parsley.

Spicy Potato & Chickpea Bites (Serves 6)

Ingredients

600g/2 1/2 cups canned chickpeas (drained & rinsed)
3 potatoes (peeled & diced)
1 1/2 onions (finely chopped)
1 fresh green chilli (finely sliced)
2 tomatoes (sliced)
2 tsps chilli powder
9 tbsps water
3 tbsps tamarind paste
3 tsps sugar
1 tsp salt

Directions

1. Place the chickpeas in a
large bowl and leave to one
side.

2. Boil the diced potatoes in a pan
of boiling water for 6-10 minutes,
until tender. Drain and leave to one
side.

3. Place the tamarind and water in bowl
and mix together. Add the sugar, chilli powder
and salt and mix well. Pour over the chickpeas.

4. Add the diced potatoes and onion and gently mix all the ingredients together,
combining them well.

5. Transfer to 6 small serving bowls and top with the sliced tomatoes and fresh
chilli.

Spiced Sweet Potato Soup (Serves 8)

Ingredients

3-4 tsps paprika

5-6 medium sweet potatoes (peeled & cut into chunks)

1 clove of garlic (crushed)

2 onions (finely chopped)

14-16 streaky bacon rashers (chopped)

2 litres/8 cups vegetable stock

5 tbsps olive oil

salt & black pepper (to season)

Directions

1. Preheat the oven to 200C/400F/Gas mark 6.

2. Place the sweet potato chunks and 3 tbsps of olive oil in a bowl and gently toss together. Transfer to a roasting tin and place in the oven for 15-20 minutes, until softened and lightly browned.

3. Add the remaining oil in a large saucepan and heat. Add the bacon and cook for 5-6 minutes, stirring frequently until crispy. Sprinkle over with paprika and cook for 40 seconds.

4. Stir in the onion and cook gently for 8-10 minutes, until softened. Add the stock and bring the mixture to a boil. Reduce the heat and simmer.

5. Carefully add the sweet potatoes and cook for a further 5-6 minutes. Remove approximately half of the sweet potato and onion mixture and place to one side. Transfer the remaining soup to a food processor (in batches) and blend until smooth.

6. Return the liquid soup to the saucepan and add the sweet potato and onion. Reheat and season with salt and black pepper, according to taste.

Spicy Potato & Tomato Chowder (Serves 4)

Ingredients

325g/12 oz potatoes (peeled & diced)
425g/1lb canned, chopped tomatoes
1 onion (chopped)
1 green pepper (finely chopped)
1 clove of garlic (crushed)
2 tsps hot chilli sauce
1 tbsp vegetable oil
salt & black pepper (to season)

Directions

1. Heat the vegetable oil in a saucepan, over a medium heat and add the garlic and onion. Cook for 4-5 minutes, until tender.

2. Add the chopped tomatoes, green pepper, potatoes and hot chilli sauce and mix all the ingredients together well. Season with salt and black pepper, according to taste. Bring to the boil.

3. Reduce the heat, cover the saucepan and simmer for 25 minutes, stirring occasionally, until the potato is cooked. Add a little more water, if required.

4. Serve hot with warm crusty bread.

Sweet Potato & Red Pepper Soup (Serves 4)

Ingredients

480g/1lb 1oz sweet potatoes (peeled & diced)
2 red peppers (deseeded & quartered)
1 red onion (sliced)
450ml/2 cups vegetable stock
1 1/2 tbsps vegetable oil
salt & black pepper (to season)
paprika (to garnish)

Directions

1. Preheat the oven to 200C/400F/Gas mark 6.

2. Place the onion and sweet potato in a roasting tin and drizzle over with the vegetable oil. Using your hands, mix the vegetables together, covering them with the oil.

3. Add the peppers and place in the oven for 40-45 minutes, until all the vegetables are tender.

4. Remove from the oven and transfer the vegetables to a food processor with a little of the vegetable stock. Process the mixture until pureed.

5. Add more of the stock and process again, repeat this process until the desired consistency is reached.

6. Transfer the soup to a saucepan and heat. Season with salt and black pepper, according to taste and serve. Top with a sprinkle of paprika.

Classic American Potato Salad (Serves 12)

Ingredients

1 1/2kg/6 1/2 cups of cooked potatoes (cubed)

3 tbsps lemon juice

375g/1 1/2 cups of mayonnaise

3 tbsps olive oil

8 tbsps leeks (chopped)

6 tbsps fresh chives (chopped)

salt & pepper (to season)

Directions

1. Place 3/4 of the diced potatoes in a large bowl. Add the lemon juice, mayonnaise and olive oil. Season with salt and black pepper and gently toss.

2. Add 3 tbsps of the chopped chives and toss again, coating the potatoes well.

3. Spoon the remaining potato over the top and sprinkle over the chopped leeks and remaining chives. Cover and refrigerate for 30-40 minutes before serving.

Creamy Potato & Pepper Salad (Serves 4)

Ingredients

450g/1lb new potatoes (scrubbed)

2 celery sticks (diced)

1/2 green pepper (deseeded & chopped into rings)

1/2 green pepper (deseeded & chopped)

1 onion (finely chopped)

1/2 large cucumber (peeled & diced)

150ml/2/3 cup sour cream

1 tsp French mustard

1/4 tsp cayenne pepper

3/4 tsp salt

Directions

1. Boil the potatoes for 12-15 minutes, until tender. Drain and set aside to cool completely. Once cooled, chop the potatoes in half.

Creamy Potato & Pepper Salad (Serves 4) cont/

2. Place the celery, onion, chopped green pepper and cucumber in a bowl and mix together. Add the potato halves and gently combine. Cover and refrigerate until ready to serve.

3. When ready to serve, place the sour cream, cayenne pepper, French mustard and salt in a small bowl and mix together well. Pour over the chilled salad and gently toss together.

4. Garnish with the green pepper rings and serve.

Egg & Potato Mayonnaise (Serves 4)

Ingredients

500g/1.1lbs new potatoes
4 hard-boiled eggs (chopped)
4 spring onions (chopped)
2 dill pickles (chopped)
2 tbsps of dill juice
3 tbsps mayonnaise
2 tbsps natural yoghurt
2 tbsps French dressing

Directions

1. Boil the potatoes for 10-12 minutes, until tender. Drain thoroughly and leave to cool a little. Chop roughly and set aside in a large bowl.

2. Pour the French dressing over the potatoes, whilst they are still warm and toss gently. Leave to cool.

3. Once cooled, add the spring onions, dill pickles and chopped eggs.

4. Place the yoghurt, mayonnaise and dill juice in a bowl and mix together well. Add to the potato and egg salad and toss gently, but thoroughly.

5. Transfer to a serving dish and serve.

Mediterranean-Style Potato Salad (Serves 4)

Ingredients - Salad

525g/1.2lbs new potatoes (scrubbed & quartered)
420g/1 3/4 cup canned chickpeas (drained & rinsed)
60g/2 1/2 oz pitted black olives (chopped)
180g/6 oz cherry tomatoes (halved)
2 red onions (thinly sliced)

Ingredients - Dressing

2 tbsps fresh lemon juice
3 tbsps olive oil
1 tsp Dijon mustard
1 tsp lemon zest (grated)
salt & black pepper (to season)

Directions

1. Boil the potatoes for 12-15 minutes, until tender. Drain and place to one side.

2. Place the olive oil, lemon juice, Dijon mustard and lemon zest in a bowl and season with salt and black pepper, according to taste. Whisk the dressing ingredients together with a fork or hand whisk.

3. Place the still-warm potatoes in a bowl and pour half of the dressing over the top. Leave to cool for 5-10 minutes.

4. Add the olives, chickpeas, onions and tomatoes to the potatoes. Pour over the remaining dressing and gently toss together. Serve immediately.

New Potato & Shallot Salad (Serves 4)

Ingredients - Salad

450g/1lb new potatoes
3 shallots (peeled & finely chopped)
2 tbsps fresh chives (snipped)
salt (to season)

Ingredients - Vinaigrette

1 clove of garlic (crushed)
1 tsp mustard powder
1/2 tbsp balsamic vinegar
1/2 tbsp sherry vinegar
5 tbsps olive oil
1 tsp sea salt (crushed)
black pepper (to season)

Directions

1. Boil the potatoes for 15-20 minutes, until just tender. Drain well and return to the pan. Leave to cool for 5-8 minutes.

2. To make the vinaigrette, crush the salt and garlic together with a pestle and mortar, until pureed. Add the mustard powder and blend in well. Transfer to a bowl.

3. Mix some black pepper into the mixture, followed by the balsamic and sherry vinegars. Pour in the olive oil and whisk all the ingredients together well, using a hand whisk.

4. Transfer the still-warm potatoes to a large bowl and stir in the shallots and vinaigrette. Add the chives and gently toss the ingredients together. Transfer to a serving bowl and serve.

Potato, Bacon & Tomato Salad (Serves 8)

Ingredients

950g/2lbs new potatoes (scrubbed & halved)
450g/1lb cherry tomatoes (halved)
12 rashers of back bacon (chopped)
2 tbsps extra virgin olive oil
2 tbsps balsamic vinegar
4 tsps honey
20g/3/4 oz parsley (chopped)
salt & black pepper (to season)

Directions

1. Boil the potatoes for 12-15 minutes, until tender. Drain and set to one side.

2. Halfway through the potatoes cooking time, fry the bacon in a frying pan for 5-6 minutes, until crispy.

3. Place the balsamic vinegar, olive oil and honey in a bowl and whisk together.

4. Stir the bacon into the potatoes, followed by the cherry tomatoes and chopped parsley. Pour over the dressing and gently toss all the ingredients together. Season with a little salt and black pepper, if desired.

5. Serve immediately.

Potato, Fennel & Carrot Salad (Serves 2-4)

Ingredients - Salad

1 large potato (cut into thin strips)

2 carrots (grated)

1 fennel bulb (cut into thin strips)

1 red onion (cut into thin strips)

2 tbsps extra-virgin olive oil

fresh chives (chopped)

Ingredients - Dressing

1 clove of garlic (crushed)

3 tbsps extra-virgin olive oil

1 tbsp garlic wine vinegar

2 tsps clear honey

1 tsp Dijon mustard

salt & black pepper (to season)

Directions

1. Place all of the ingredients in a bowl and whisk together and set aside.

2. For the salad, heat the oil in a frying pan and add the fennel and potato. Cook for 3-4 minutes, until lightly browned. Remove with a slotted spoon and drain on paper kitchen towel.

3. Arrange the red onion, carrot, potato and fennel on serving plates. Pour over the dressing and gently toss together. Sprinkle with chopped chives and serve, or cover and chill until ready to serve.

Salad Nicoise (Serves 4-6)

Ingredients

10 new potatoes (diced)

1 bag of mixed salad

2 tomatoes

2 hard-boiled eggs (sliced)

2 x 175g cans of tuna in water

1 x 400g can of artichokes (drained, rinsed and chopped)

450g/2 cups of frozen green beans (cooked and drained)

Directions

1. Boil the diced potatoes in boiling water for 10-15 minutes. Drain them and leave to cool for 10 minutes.

2. Arrange all the ingredients equally onto individual serving plates and add the potatoes. Serve immediately.

Potato & Prawn Salad (Serves 4)

Ingredients

450g/1lb new potatoes
120g/4oz peeled, cooked prawns (chopped)
2 eggs (hard boiled & chopped)
1/2 cucumber (thinly sliced)
3 tbsps mayonnaise
1/2 tsp dried tarragon
Salt & black pepper (to season)

Directions

1. Boil the potatoes for 12-15 minutes, until tender. Drain and set aside to cool a little. Peel and chop the potatoes in half.

2. Place the mayonnaise and tarragon in a small container and mix together. Season a little with salt and black pepper and then mix into the still-warm potatoes. Leave to cool completely.

3. Add the chopped prawns and eggs to the potatoes and gently combine together. Arrange the cucumber around the outer rim of a large serving dish and serve the salad in the centre.

Walnut and Potato Salad (serves 4)

Ingredients

2 tbsps walnut pieces (optional)

2 tsps Dijon mustard

1 tbsp tarragon or cider vinegar

2 tbsps olive oil

2 tbsps walnut oil

1 tsp honey

flaked sea salt and freshly ground black pepper

900g/2lb new potatoes, washed or scrubbed

1 tbsp chopped fresh tarragon leaves

1 large shallot, finely chopped

2 tbsps chopped gherkins (optional)

Directions

1. Place the walnuts in a hot oven (about 200C/400F/Gas 6) for a few minutes until they begin to colour slightly.

2. Put the mustard, vinegar, honey, oils and salt and pepper in a screw-top jar. Shake the jar well until creamy. Add more seasoning if you prefer.

3. Cook the potatoes in boiling salted water for about 15-20 minutes until just tender. Drain well and, when just cool enough to handle, cut into halves or quarters, if quite large.

4. Place the potatoes in a mixing bowl with the tarragon, shallots, gherkins and walnuts, and mix in as much or as little of the dressing as you want.

5. Serve just warm or you can store it in the refrigerator, but let it warm up to room temperature before serving.

Baked Jackets with Smoked Haddock (Serves 2)

Ingredients

2 large potatoes (scrubbed & pricked with a fork)
225g/8 oz smoked haddock fillets
300ml/1 1/2 cups milk
50g/2 oz mature Cheddar cheese
40g/1 1/2 oz butter
1/2 tbsp plain flour
2 black peppercorns
salt & black pepper (to season)

Directions

1. Preheat the oven to 200C/400F/Gas mark 6. Bake the potatoes in the oven for 1 1/4-1 1/2 hours, until soft.

2. Whilst the potatoes are cooking, place the fish in a frying pan and add the whole peppercorns and milk. Bring to the boil. Reduce the heat and simmer for 8-10 minutes, until the fish flakes easily with a fork.

3. Remove the fillets from the frying pan and place on a plate. Strain the liquid from the pan using a sieve and retain the milk. Cut the fish into large chunks, removing any bones and skin. Place the fish in a bowl.

4. Melt 20g of the butter in a saucepan and add the flour. Cook for 1-2 minutes, stirring continuously. Remove from the heat and stir in the reserved milk.

5. Return the saucepan to the heat and bring to a simmer. Cook until smooth and thickened. Pour half of the sauce over the fish and gently combine, covering the chunks evenly. Add the cheese to the remaining sauce, stirring it in well until melted.

6. Remove the potatoes from the oven and set aside to cool a little. When hot enough to handle, cut the potatoes lengthways and scoop out the potato, placing the potato in a bowl and reserving the potato skins. Add the remaining butter to the cheese sauce and pour over the potatoes. Mash together well and season with salt and black pepper, according to taste.

Baked Jackets with Smoked Haddock cont/.

7. Grease an ovenproof dish.

8. Spoon the fish mixture equally into the potato skins, topped with the potato and cheese sauce mash. Place the potato skins into the ovenproof dish and place back in the oven for 8-10 minutes. Serve immediately, topped with a little butter if desired.

Cabbage & Potato Cakes with Poached Eggs (Serves 4)

Ingredients

8 medium eggs
55g/1/4 cup of unsalted butter
900g/2lb packet of mashed potato
1 clove of garlic (crushed)
1 1/2 onions (sliced)
250g/1 cup of green cabbage (shredded)
1 tsp caraway seeds
4 tbsps plain flour
40g/1 1/2 oz fresh flat-leaf parsley (chopped)

Directions

1. Cook the shredded cabbage for 3 minutes, until just tender. Drain well.

2. Melt the butter in a large frying pan and add the garlic, onion and caraway seeds. Cook for 4-5 minutes, until softened.

3. Make up the mashed potato, as per the packet instructions and mix in the cabbage.

4. Remove the onion from the frying pan with a slotted spoon and mix into the potato. Reserve the butter in the pan.

5. Add the flour and parsley to the potato mixture and combine all the ingredients well. Season, according to taste.

6. Dipping your hands in flour, divide the mixture into 8 and shape into patty-shaped rounds.

7. Reheat the butter in the frying pan and add the 8 cakes. Cook for 4-5 minutes, each side, until golden brown. Remove from the pan and keep warm.

8. Poach the eggs in simmering water and remove with a slotted spoon.

9. Place 2 potato cakes on each plate and top each with a poached egg. Sprinkle the tops with chopped parsley and serve immediately.

Creamy Chicken Jackets (Serves 4)

Ingredients
4 baking potatoes (scrubbed & pricked with a fork)
400g/1 lb cooked chicken breast (diced)
300ml/1 1/4 cups condensed cream of chicken soup
50g/2 oz frozen peas
30g/1 oz butter
1/2 tsp lemon juice
1/2 tsp dried tarragon
1/4 tsp dried thyme

Directions
1. Preheat the oven to 200C/400F/Gas mark 6. Bake the potatoes in the oven for 1 1/4-1 1/2 hours, until soft.

2. Cook the peas in boiling water for 5 minutes and drain. Place the soup in a saucepan and add the herbs, peas, chicken and lemon juice. Season with salt and black pepper, according to taste. Cook on a low heat for 10-15 minutes, until heated through.

3. Cut a lid from the top of each potato and scoop out some of the potato flesh, placing it in a bowl. Add the butter to the potato and mash together. Scoop the mashed potato back into the top of each jacket.

4. Spoon the creamy chicken sauce over the top of each jacket potato and serve immediately.

Fish & Potato Cakes with Hot Sauce (Serves 4)

Ingredients - Fishcakes

450g/1lb potatoes (diced)
225g/8oz trout fillet
225g/8oz haddock fillet
430ml/3 cups fish stock
80g/3oz dry white breadcrumbs
2 tbsps fromage frais
3 tbsps fresh chives (chopped)
1 bay leaf
1-2 tbsps vegetable oil
salt & black pepper (to season)

Ingredients - Sauce

1-2 tsps chilli powder
200ml/3/4 cup passata (sieved tomatoes)
4 tbsps dry white wine
4 tbsps natural yoghurt (unsweetened)

Directions - Fishcakes

1. Boil the potatoes for 10-12 minutes, until tender. Drain thoroughly and mash. Set aside.

2. Place both sets of fish in a large saucepan, with the fish stock and bay leaf. Bring to the boil.

3. Reduce the heat and simmer for 8-9 minutes. Remove with a slotted spoon and flake the fish away from the skin, using a fork.

4. Place the flaked fish, mashed potato, fromage frais and chives in a large bowl and combine together. Season with salt and black pepper, according to taste. Leave to cool.

5. Cover the mixture and place in the refrigerator for 1-2 hours.

6. Place the breadcrumbs on a plate. Remove the fish mixture from the refrigerator and divide into 8 equal-sized pieces. Shape each piece into a patty-shape and coat with the breadcrumbs.

7. Heat the vegetable oil in a frying pan and add the fishcakes. Cook over a medium heat for 5-6 minutes each side, until golden brown.

Directions - Sauce

1. Whilst the fishcakes are cooking, make the sauce by pouring the white wine and passata into a saucepan and heating through. Season with salt and black pepper.

2. Remove from the heat and gradually stir in the yoghurt. Return to the heat and stir in the chilli powder. Heat for 2-3 minutes.

3. Serve with the freshly cooked fishcakes and a green salad.

Leek & Cheddar Stuffed Potato Jackets (Serves 4)

Ingredients

4 large baked potatoes (already baked)
2 leeks (trimmed & cut into 1/4 inch slices)
90g/3 1/2oz mature Cheddar cheese
160g/5 1/2oz garlic & herb soft cheese
2 tbsps single cream
salt & black pepper (to season)

Directions

1. Preheat the oven to 180C/350F/Gas mark 4.

2. Place the garlic & herb cheese in a large bowl.

3. Cut the baked potatoes in half, lengthways. Carefully, scoop out the insides of the potatoes and add them to the bowl. Retain each of the skins.

4. Add the single cream and season with salt and black pepper, according to taste. Mash all of the ingredients together well. Scoop the mashed mixture out with a spoon and pile back into the potato skins.

Leek & Cheddar Stuffed Potato Jackets cont/.

5. Top each of the potatoes with leeks and cheddar cheese; pressing down the tops lightly with your palms. Place on a baking tray and place in the oven for 20-25 minutes, until the leeks are browning around the edges.
Serve immediately.

Leek & Sweet Potato Cakes (Serves 2)

Ingredients

450g/1 lb sweet potato (peeled & cut into 3/4 inch pieces)
1 leek (trimmed & finely chopped)
100g/2/3 cup canned sweetcorn (drained)
1 clove of garlic (crushed)
1/2 inch piece of fresh ginger (finely chopped)
1 tbsp fromage frais
30g/1 oz wholemeal flour
1 1/2 tbsps vegetable oil
salt & black pepper (to season)

Directions

1. Boil the potatoes for 12-15 minutes, until tender. Drain thoroughly and mash. Set aside to cool in a large bowl to cool.

2. Heat half of the vegetable oil in a frying pan and add the garlic, ginger and leeks. Cook for 3-4 minutes. Remove with a slotted spoon and mix into the mashed potato.

3. Stir in the sweetcorn and fromage frais and season with salt and black pepper, according to taste. Combine well.

4. Place the flour on a plate.

5. Form the mixture into 4 equally-sized patty-shapes and coat in the flour. Cover and place in the refrigerator for 30-40 minutes.

6. Preheat the grill to a medium heat and lightly brush each of the cakes with vegetable oil. Grill for 5-6 minutes on each side, until golden brown. Drain off any excess fat on paper kitchen towel. Serve hot with a green side salad.

Potato & Asparagus Quiche (Serves 4-6)

Ingredients

1 large potato (peeled & grated)
180g/6oz short potato pastry
425g/1 3/4 cups canned asparagus
150ml/1/2 cup single cream
3 eggs (beaten)
salt & black pepper (to season)

Directions

1. Preheat the oven to 180C/350F/Gas mark 4. Grease an 8 inch round baking tin and line it with the pastry. Place in the oven for 15-20 minutes, until golden brown.

2. Remove from the oven and leave to cool a little. Increase the heat of the oven to 220C/425F/Gas mark 7.

3. Place the potato, single cream and beaten eggs in a bowl; season with salt and black pepper and mix together. Pour the mixture into the quiche base and place the asparagus spears in a circle (tips inwards towards the centre, ends towards the edge of the pastry). Return to the oven and cook for 10 minutes.

4. Reduce the heat to 180C/350F/Gas mark 4 and cook for a further 25-30 minutes, until the quiche is set.

5. Serve hot or cold.

Potato & Vegetable Patties (Serves 3-4)

Ingredients

500g/2 cups potato (peeled and cubed)
280g/1 1/4 cups carrots (peeled and finely chopped)
170g/3/4 cup of frozen peas
2 spring onions (finely chopped)
1 egg
pinch of salt and pepper

Directions

1. Add the potato cubes to a pan and boil until tender (approximately 5 minutes). Add the carrots and peas to a pan and boil until tender (approximately 3-4 minutes).

2. Mash the potatoes in a bowl and mix in the peas, carrots and spring onions. Beat the egg and add to the mixture, with a pinch of salt and pepper.

3. Place the ingredients into a food processor and blend until the mixture is slightly 'chunky'.

4. Remove from the processor and make the mixture into individual patties. Place under the grill until golden brown on both sides. Serve with either a side salad, or in a bun.

Spinach & Potato Patties (Serves 2-4)

Ingredients

500g/3 1/3 cups potatoes (boiled & mashed)
275g/2 3/4 cups frozen spinach (thawed, drained, dried & chopped)
1 onion (chopped)
125g/1 cup Cheddar cheese (grated)
1 clove of garlic (crushed)
1 tbsp vegetable oil
1/4 tsp ground nutmeg
salt & black pepper (to season)
wholewheat flour (for coating)
vegetable oil (for shallow frying)

Directions

1. Heat the 1 tbsp of vegetable oil in a saucepan and add the garlic and onion. Cook for 4-5 minutes, until tender.

2. Add the mashed potatoes, spinach, cheese and nutmeg to the saucepan. Season with salt and black pepper and mix together well.

3. Using slightly dampened hands, shape the mixture into balls and then flatten them a little with the palm of your hand.

4. Place some wholewheat flour on a plate and coat each of the patties evenly, on both sides.

5. Heat enough oil for shallow frying in a frying pan and add the patties. Fry for 2-3 minutes, each side, until browned. Remove and drain on paper kitchen towel. Serve hot with warm crusty bread and a side salad.

Veggie-Filled Jacket Potatoes (Serves 1)

Ingredients

1 jacket potato
110g/1/2 cup of canned, chopped tomatoes
1/4 onion (finely chopped)
1/4 aubergine (chopped)
1/4 courgette (chopped)
1/4 red pepper (chopped)
1 tbsp olive oil
Handful of grated cheese (optional)

Directions

1. Place the potato on a microwavable dish and cook on high for 8-10 minutes; or, for microwaves with specific programmes for potatoes, set the appropriate weight and cook.

2. Whilst the potato is cooking, heat the olive oil in a frying pan and add the chopped vegetables and tomatoes. Bring to the boil, reduce the heat and summer for 3-5 minutes, until the vegetables are soft.

Veggie-Filled Jacket Potatoes cont/.

3. Split the cooked potato and fill with the hot vegetable mixture. Sprinkle with a little grated cheese, if desired.

Zesty Tuna Jackets (Makes 8)

Ingredients

6 jacket potatoes (scrubbed & dried)
4-5 cans of tuna (drained)
2 red peppers (finely chopped)
juice of 2 limes
handful of fresh coriander leaves (chopped)

Directions

1. Preheat the oven to 200C/400F/Gas mark 6.

2. Prick each of the potatoes with a fork or sharp knife. Rub a little olive oil over each potato and sprinkle with rock salt.

3. Place the potatoes in the oven and bake for 1 1/4 to 1 1/2 hours, until soft inside.

4. Place the tuna into a bowl and add the lime juice, chopped coriander and red pepper. Mix together gently, but well.

5. Open the potatoes and spoon the tuna mixture on top of each. Season with black pepper, according to taste.

Bolton Hot-Pot (Serves 4-6)

Ingredients

700g/4 2/3 cups potatoes (peeled & thinly sliced)
4 large lamb chops (trimmed of fat)
4 lambs' kidneys (skinned, cored & sliced)
1 large onion (chopped)
120g/4 1/2 oz button mushrooms
6-8 smoked oysters
225ml/1 cup meat stock
50g/1/4 cup lard
Salt & black pepper (to season)

Directions

1. Preheat the oven to 160C/325F/Gas mark 3.

2. Keep the potato slices immersed in cold water, to ensure that they don't discolour.

3. Heat the lamb chops in a frying pan for 2-3 minutes each side. Remove and transfer to an ovenproof casserole dish, in one layer.

4. Top the lamb chops with half of the onion and a layer of potato slices (patting them dry with paper kitchen towel first). Season with salt and black pepper, according to taste.

5. Place the kidney slices in the same frying pan that the chops were cooked in and cook over a high heat for 1-2 minutes. Spoon into the casserole dish, spreading them out evenly.

6. Melt 15g of the lard in the frying pan and add the mushrooms. Cook for 1-2 minutes, stirring frequently. Transfer to the casserole dish, followed by the oysters and remaining onion. Season a little with salt and black pepper and pour over the stock.

7. Drain and dry the remaining potato slices and arrange over the top, overlapping them at the sides.

Bolton Hot-Pot cont/.

8. Melt the remaining lard and brush it over the top of the potatoes. Cover with a lid and place in the oven for 55-60 minutes, until the potatoes are tender.

9. Increase the heat to 220C/425F/Gas Mark 7 and remove the casserole dish lid. Return to the oven and cook for 25-30 minutes, until golden brown.

10. Serve piping hot with seasonal vegetables.

Bubble and Squeak (Serves 4)

Ingredients

450g/2 cups potatoes (peeled & boiled)
110g/1/2 cup of chopped bacon
225g/1 cup of cabbage or brussel sprouts (cooked & shredded)
55g/1/4 cup of butter
1 tbsp chopped parsley
3 tbsps vegetable oil
pinch of black pepper

Directions

1. Once the potatoes have been boiled, drain and add in the butter and black pepper. Mash the potatoes.

2. Fry the chopped bacon until crispy and then stir into the mash. Add in the cabbage or sprouts, along with the parsley. Shape the mix into 4 balls and flatten down to about 2 inch-high cakes.

3. Heat the oil in a frying pan and fry each of the cakes for 3-4 minutes on each side – until golden brown. Serve with a side salad.

Carrot & Potato Souffle (Serves 4)

Ingredients

375g/13oz potatoes (cut into 1/2 inch/1cm pieces)

450g/16oz carrots (cut into 1 inch/2.5cm pieces)

5 eggs (separated)

120g/1 cup mature Cheddar cheese (grated)

4-5 tsps French mustard

2 tbsps milk

30g/1oz butter

salt & black pepper (to season)

Directions

1. Preheat the oven to 200C/400F/Gas mark 6. Grease a 1.5 litre soufflé dish.

2. Boil the carrots gently in salted water, for 12-15 minutes, until tender. Boil the potatoes for 10-12 minutes, until tender. Drain well and transfer the potatoes and carrots to a large, clean saucepan.

3. Mash the carrots and potatoes with the milk and butter, until smooth. Transfer to a large bowl.

4. Stir in the egg yolks, grated cheese and mustard. Season with salt and black pepper and beat together with a wooden spoon.

5. Place the egg whites in a bowl and whisk until soft peaks are formed. Gradually fold them into the carrot/potato mixture, using a large metal spoon.

6. Transfer the mixture to the soufflé dish and place in the oven for 30-35 minutes, until cooked and risen.

Cheese & Potato Casserole with Sour Cream (Serves 4-6)

Ingredients

6 medium potatoes (grated)
120g/1 cup of Cheddar cheese (grated)
225ml/1 cup of sour cream
Bunch of spring onions (chopped)
115g/1/2 cup of butter (melted)
1-2 tsps salt
black pepper (to season)

Directions

1. Preheat the oven to 220C/425F/Gas mark 7. Grease a large casserole dish.

2. Place the potatoes, spring onions, salt, sour cream and cheese in a large bowl and combine well.

3. Transfer the mixture to the casserole dish, spreading it evenly. Pour the melted butter over the top of the casserole and season with a little black pepper.

4. Place in the oven for 25-30 minutes, until the potatoes are cooked and browned.

5. Serve hot.

Corned Beef & Potato Hash (Serves 4)

Ingredients

700g/9 cups potatoes (cubed)
350g/12oz canned, corned beef (diced)
180g/6oz canned, sweetcorn (drained)
1 onion (chopped)
1 red pepper (diced)
2 tsps Worcestershire sauce
2 tbsps vegetable oil
1 tbsp fresh parsley (chopped)
salt & black pepper (to season)

Directions

1. Boil the potatoes for 12-15 minutes, until tender. Drain and set to one side.

2. Heat the oil in a frying pan and add the potatoes and sauté for 8-10 minutes, until golden brown. Add the red pepper and onion and cook for 5-6 minutes. Remove from the heat.

3. Add the sweetcorn, corned beef and Worcestershire sauce. Season with salt and black pepper, according to taste.

4. Return to the heat and cook for 8-10 minutes, until heated through. Serve immediately, sprinkled with a little chopped parsley.

Dry Potato Curry (Serves 4-6)

Ingredients

650g/8 cups waxy potatoes (cut into 2cm chunks)
1 large onion (finely sliced)
1 tsp cumin
1 tsp turmeric
1 tsp cayenne pepper
1 tsp mustard seeds
2 cloves of garlic (crushed)
1 inch piece of fresh root ginger (grated)
1 fresh green chilli (deseeded & chopped)
2 tbsps vegetable oil

Directions

1. Boil the potatoes for 8-10 minutes, until just tender – drain and set aside.

2. Heat the vegetable oil in a large saucepan and add the mustard seeds and cook for 30-40 seconds, until they begin to pop. Add the onion and cook for 4-5 minutes, until tender.

3. Stir in the ginger and garlic and cook for 1 minute. Add the chilli, turmeric, cumin, cayenne pepper and potato chunks and combine well. Cover the saucepan and cook for 4-5 minutes, stirring occasionally. Once the potatoes are tender and flavoured well with spices, transfer to a serving dish and serve immediately.

Herbed Potato Cake (Serves 4-6)

Ingredients

720g/5 cups potatoes (grated & soaked in water for 1 hour)
100g/3/4 cup wholemeal flour
1 garlic clove (crushed)
1 large onion
1 large egg (beaten)
1 tsp bicarbonate of soda
2 tbsps fresh parsley (chopped)
50g/1/4 cup butter
Salt & black pepper (to season)

Directions

1. Preheat the oven to 180C/350F/Gas mark 4. Grease a 10 inch/25.5 cm flan tin.

2. Drain the soaked potatoes using a colander, pressing out any excess water. Pat dry with a paper kitchen towel.

3. Melt 25g/1oz of the butter in a frying pan and add the garlic and onion. Cook for 5-6 minutes, until tender. Add the remaining butter, melt and remove from the heat.

4. Sift the flour and bicarbonate of soda in a shallow bowl and season with salt and black pepper, mix together.

5. Place the grated potatoes in a bowl and stir in the flour mixture, followed by the herbs and onion/garlic mixture – combine well. Mix in the beaten egg.

6. Transfer the mixture to the flan tin and place in the oven for 50-60 minutes, until browned and cooked through. Serve immediately.

Hot Beef & Potato Supper (Serves 2)

Ingredients

2 tsps paprika

1 tbsp fresh chives (chopped)

225g/1 1/2 cups of rump or sirloin steak (cut into 1 inch long strips)

170g/3/4 cup of cooked new potatoes (halved)

1 red onion (sliced)

300ml/1 1/3 cups beef stock (hot)

70g/1/3 cup of cherry tomatoes (halved)

1 clove of garlic (crushed)

30g/1/4 cup of plain flour

1 tbsp vegetable oil

splash of Worcestershire sauce

salt & black pepper (to season)

Directions

1. Place the flour in a bowl and add the paprika, mix together well. Toss the strips of beef in the mixture, coating them well and place to one side.

2. Heat the vegetable oil in a large frying pan and add the coated beef strips. Cook for 3-4 minutes, stirring occasionally to brown all sides of the meat.

3. Add the garlic, potatoes and onion and continue to cook for 3 minutes. Add the beef stock, cherry tomatoes and Worcestershire sauce and season with salt and black pepper, according to taste. Cook for a further 2-3 minutes.

4. Adjust seasoning, if required and sprinkle over with chopped chives. Serve hot with warm, crusty bread and a choice of vegetables.

Hot-Pot-Lamb-Chops (Serves 4)

Ingredients

4 boneless lamb steaks (trimmed & lightly seasoned)
1 large potato (thinly sliced)
1 carrot (thinly sliced)
1 small onion (thinly sliced)
1 tsp dried rosemary
1-2 tsps olive oil
salt & black pepper (to season)
fresh rosemary sprigs (to garnish)

Directions

1. Preheat the oven to 180C/350F/Gas mark 4.

2. Place the seasoned lamb steaks on a baking tray and alternate layers of sliced onion, carrot and then potato on top of each steak.

3. Brush the top of each with olive oil and season with salt and black pepper, according to taste. Sprinkle the top with dried rosemary.

4. Place in the oven for 25-30 minutes, until the lamb is cooked and tender.

5. Remove from the oven and drain on paper kitchen towel. Transfer to serving plates and top with fresh rosemary.

6. Serve immediately with a choice of green vegetables.

Lemon Chicken & Potato Wedge Bake (Serves 4-6)

Ingredients

525g/1lb 3oz potatoes (scrubbed & cut into wedges)
6 chicken breasts (with skins)
4 cloves of garlic (whole)
1 clove of garlic (crushed)
1 lemon (zest removed & cut in half)
1 red onion (cut into wedges)
1 1/2 tsps clear honey
1 tsp fresh thyme
5 sprigs of fresh rosemary
2 tbsps olive oil
salt & black pepper (to season)

Directions

1. Preheat the oven to 180C/350F/Gas mark 4.

2. Heat a non-stick frying pan and add the chicken breasts, skin-side down. Cook for 3-4 minutes over a medium heat, until the skin is browned. Transfer to a large roasting tin.

3. Add the potato wedges and onion to the roasting tin, distributing them evenly around the chicken breasts.

4. Cut one half of the lemon into wedges and add them to the roasting tin, with the 4 whole cloves of garlic.

5. Squeeze the juice from the other half of the lemon into a mixing jug and add the olive oil, honey and crushed garlic. Mix together and pour evenly over the chicken and potatoes.

6. Season with salt and black pepper, according to taste and add the thyme and rosemary.

7. Place in the oven and bake for 50-60 minutes until the chicken is cooked through and the potatoes are tender and golden. Serve immediately.

Mexican-Style Chicken & Potatoes (Serves 4)

Ingredients

725g/5 cups potatoes (peeled & diced)
4 chicken breasts (cubed)
425g/1 2/3 cups canned, chopped tomatoes
420g/2 1/2 cups canned, black beans (drained & rinsed)
1 red pepper (chopped)
1 onion (chopped)
2-3 tsps Chipotle paste
1 tbsp olive oil
150ml/5fl oz water

Directions

1. Preheat the oven to
200C/400F/Gas mark 6.

2. Heat the oil in a frying pan
and add the chicken. Cook for
2-3 minutes, sealing the chicken.
Add the onion and diced potatoes
and cook for 5-6 minutes.

3. Stir in the Chipotle paste and add the black
beans, chopped tomatoes and red pepper. Mix
together well. Add the water and bring to the boil.

4. Transfer the mixture to a casserole dish, cover and place in the oven and bake for
40-45 minutes, stirring twice during. Check that the potatoes and chicken are
cooked through. Serve hot.

Potato & Aduki Bean Pie (Serves 8)

Ingredients

250g/1 1/2 cups of aduki beans (soaked overnight, drained & rinsed)
875g/5 cups of potatoes (peeled)
450g/3 cups of carrots (diced)
1 onion (finely chopped)
4 tbsps tomato puree
55g/1/4 cup of butter
3 tbsps soy sauce
1 1/2 tsps dried mixed herbs
1 tbsp vegetable oil
salt & black pepper

Directions

1. Preheat the oven to 180C/350F/Gas mark 4.

2. Place the rinsed and drained aduki beans in a large saucepan and cover with water (3 pints). Bring to the boil, reduce the heat and simmer for 50 minutes. Drain the beans, reserving the liquid.

3. Heat the oil in a large frying pan and add the onion. Cook for 4-5 minutes, until clear. Add the carrots and cook for 3-4 minutes, followed by the cooked aduki beans.

4. Place the tomato puree, herbs and soy sauce in a large bowl and mix together. Stir in the reserved bean stock and then pour over the bean/vegetable mixture. Bring back to the boil, reduce the heat and simmer for 20-25 minutes. Season with salt and black pepper and transfer to a large heatproof casserole dish.

5. Whilst the bean/vegetable mixture is simmering, boil the potatoes until ready to mash. Add the butter and mash well. Spread the mashed potatoes evenly over the bean/vegetable mixture

6. Place in the oven and bake for 25-30 minutes, until the topping is golden brown.

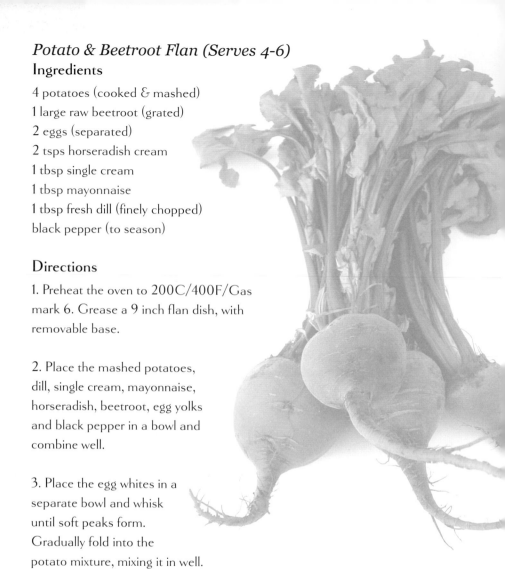

Potato & Beetroot Flan (Serves 4-6)

Ingredients

4 potatoes (cooked & mashed)
1 large raw beetroot (grated)
2 eggs (separated)
2 tsps horseradish cream
1 tbsp single cream
1 tbsp mayonnaise
1 tbsp fresh dill (finely chopped)
black pepper (to season)

Directions

1. Preheat the oven to 200C/400F/Gas mark 6. Grease a 9 inch flan dish, with removable base.

2. Place the mashed potatoes, dill, single cream, mayonnaise, horseradish, beetroot, egg yolks and black pepper in a bowl and combine well.

3. Place the egg whites in a separate bowl and whisk until soft peaks form. Gradually fold into the potato mixture, mixing it in well.

4. Spoon the mixture into the flan dish and place in the oven for 25-30 minutes, until cooked and firm.

5. Remove from the oven and leave to cool for 2-3 minutes. Slice into wedges and serve.

Potato & Cheese Bake (Serves 4)
Ingredients - Bake
1kg/2lbs 4oz waxy potatoes (peeled & cut into 1/4 inch slices)
100g/4oz Cheddar cheese (grated)

Ingredients - Sauce
850g/3 1/2 cups canned, chopped tomatoes (with juices)
2 tbsps tomato puree
250g/9oz button mushrooms (sliced)
2 cloves of garlic (crushed)
1 large onion (finely chopped)
1 tbsp olive oil
salt & black pepper (to season)

Directions
1. Boil the potato slices for 10-12 minutes, until just tender. Drain and set to one side.

2. To make the sauce, heat the olive oil in a saucepan and add the garlic and onion. Cook over a medium heat for 5-6 minutes, until tender. Stir in the tomato puree, followed by the canned tomatoes. Cook for 1 minute.

3. Add the mushrooms and continue to cook, uncovered, for 12-15 minutes, until the liquid has reduced right down. Season with salt and black pepper, according to taste. Remove from the heat.

4. Preheat the grill to a medium/high heat.

5. Lightly grease a heatproof dish (one that will fit underneath the grill) and layer half of the potato slices inside the base. Carefully spoon the sauce over the top and sprinkle over with half of the grated cheese.

6. Layer the remaining potatoes over the top and sprinkle over the rest of the cheese. Place under the grill for 5-7 minutes, until heated through and the cheese is golden brown.

7. Serve immediately with a choice of green vegetables.

Potato & Vegetable Pizza (Serves 2-4)

Ingredients - Pizza Base

250g/1 1/4 cups cold mashed potatoes

110g/3/4 cup self-raising flour

50g/1/4 cup butter

vegetable oil (for greasing)

Ingredients - Topping

200g/1 2/3 cups mature Cheddar cheese (grated)

130g/4 1/2oz button mushrooms (sliced)

1 red pepper (deseeded & sliced)

1 large onion (sliced)

1 clove of garlic (crushed)

1 1/4 tbsps tomato puree

1 tbsp vegetable oil

1 1/2 tsps malt vinegar

1/4 tsp oregano

salt & black pepper (to season)

Directions

1. Preheat the oven to 230C/450F/Gas mark 8. Grease a large baking sheet with vegetable oil.

Directions - Pizza Base

1. Sift the salt and flour into a large bowl and add the butter, rubbing it in with your fingers, until it forms a breadcrumb-like mixture.

2. Add the mashed potatoes and knead the mixture lightly, until well combined and smooth. Press into a 10inch round and place in the refrigerator for 20-30 minutes.

Directions - Topping

1. Heat the vegetable oil in a frying pan and add the onions, garlic and red pepper. Cook for 4-5 minutes, until tender and slightly golden. Remove from the heat.

2. Stir in the vinegar, oregano and mushrooms and season with salt and black pepper, according to taste.

3. Remove the potato base from the refrigerator and place on the baking sheet. Spread the top with tomato puree and then top with the mushroom/onion mixture.

4. Sprinkle cheese evenly over the top and place in the oven for 25-30 minutes, until the base is firm and the cheese is golden brown.

Prawn & Potato Curry (Serves 6)

Ingredients

900g/2lbs potatoes (peeled & diced)
420g/13oz tiger prawns (cooked & peeled)
130g frozen peas (defrosted)
260m/l 1/4 cups milk
400ml/1 3/4 cups canned coconut milk
1 onion (chopped)
2 tbsps Thai green curry paste
1/2 lemongrass stalk (finely chopped)
1 tbsp olive oil
salt & black pepper (to season)

Directions

1. Heat the oil in a large saucepan and add the potatoes and onion. Cook over a medium heat for 5-6 minutes. Stir in the Thai curry paste and lemongrass and cook for 1-2 minutes, stirring frequently.

2. Add the milk and coconut milk and bring to the boil. Reduce the heat and simmer for 20-25 minutes, until the potatoes are tender.

3. Add the prawns and peas and cook for 3-4 minutes, heating them through.

4. Season with salt and black pepper, according to taste. Serve immediately with boiled rice or freshly cooked noodles.

Slow-Cook Thai Pumpkin & Sweet Potato Curry (Serves 4-6)

Ingredients

500g/4 1/3 cups pumpkin (deseeded & diced)
275g/1 1/2 cups sweet potato (peeled & diced)
125g/1 1/4 cups of chestnut mushrooms (sliced)
125g/1 cup of roasted peanuts (chopped)
335ml/1 1/2 cups of coconut milk
395ml/1 3/4 cups of hot vegetable stock
3 cloves of garlic (crushed)
4 shallots (finely chopped)
1 inch of fresh galangal (finely chopped)
2 tbsps vegetable oil
2 tbsps Thai fish sauce
2 tbsps yellow curry paste
1 tbsp soy sauce
3 kaffir lime leaves (shredded)
55g/2oz pumpkin seeds (toasted)

Directions

To be cooked in a slow cooker.

1. Heat the vegetable oil in a large frying pan and
add the shallots and garlic. Cook for 8-10 minutes, over
a medium heat, until lightly browned.

2. Stir in the yellow curry paste and stir-fry for 30-40 seconds. Transfer the mixture
into the slow cooker's ceramic pot.

3. Add the galangal, sweet potatoes, pumpkin and lime leaves to the pot, followed
by half of the coconut milk. Gently stir the ingredients together, combing them well.
Cover and cook on a high setting for 1 1/4-1 1/2 hours.

4. Add the mushrooms, Thai fish sauce, soy sauce and chopped peanuts to the
curry, stirring them in well. Pour in the remaining coconut milk and re-cover. Cook
on high for 2 1/2-3 hours, until all the vegetables are tender.

5. Serve in bowls, garnished with a sprinkling of pumpkin seeds.

Spicy Pan Fried Potatoes & Beef (Serves 4)

Ingredients

2 large potatoes (peeled & cut into small chunks)

420g/15oz beef fillet (thickly sliced & cut into small cubes)

3 cloves of garlic (peeled & slightly crushed down)

2 yellow peppers (deseeded & cut into thick slices)

1 red chilli pepper (finely chopped)

4 tbsps extra-virgin olive oil

2 tbsps light olive oil

1 tbsp parsley (finely chopped)

1/4 tsp oregano

salt & black pepper (to season)

Directions

1. Boil the potatoes in salted water for 5 minutes. Drain and set aside to cool.

2. Heat the extra-virgin olive oil in a large frying pan and add the whole garlic cloves and sliced peppers. Add the oregano, the chilli peppers and half of the chopped parsley. Cook over a medium/high heat for 2-3 minutes.

3. Add a little salt and stir and cook for 1 minute. Reduce the heat to a low setting and stir in the potatoes and cover the pan. Cook for 10 minutes, stirring occasionally.

4. Season the beef with salt and black pepper. Heat the light olive oil in a large frying pan and add the beef. Stir-fry for 1-2 minutes. Add the potato mixture to the frying pan and stir together well. Remove from the heat.

5. Top with the remaining parsley and serve immediately.

Sweet Potato & Chickpea Stew (Serves 4)

Ingredients

100g/1/2 cup of dried chickpeas
785ml/3 1/2 cups of water
1 sweet potato
1 carrot (sliced)
225g/1 cup of broccoli florets
1/2 celery stick (sliced)
1/2 onion (chopped)
1/2 leek (sliced)
1 tsp horseradish sauce
1/4 tsp hot pepper sauce
1/2 tsp ground cumin
1/2 tsp ground coriander
1 tsp soy sauce
1/2 tbsp lemon juice
1 tbsp vegetable oil

Directions

To be cooked in a slow cooker.

1. Place the chickpeas in a large pan with the water and soak overnight.

2. Heat the slow cooker to a high temperature.

3. Heat the oil in a frying pan and add the onion. Cook for 4-5 minutes, until tender. Place in the slow cooker.

4. Add all of the remaining ingredients to the slow cooker and mix together well. Cover and cook for 7 to 9 hours, until the vegetables are tender and the chickpeas are cooked.

5. Serve in individual serving bowls with warm, crusty bread.

Sweet Potato & Vegetable Shepherd's Pie (Serves 4)

Ingredients

4 sweet potatoes

1 butternut squash (diced)

2 carrots (sliced)

1 broccoli head (finely chopped)

1 courgette (sliced)

3 tomatoes (halved)

1 red pepper

2 tsps olive oil

1 garlic clove (crushed)

1 onion (sliced)

2 stalks celery (sliced)

1 bay leaf

450ml/2 cups of vegetable stock

400g/1 1/2 cups (1 can) of red kidney beans (rinsed)

1 tsp arrowroot

Directions

1. Preheat the oven to 200C/400F/Gas mark 6.

2. Peel and cut the sweet potato into large cubes. Boil for 12-15 minutes, until soft. Mash the potato and place to one side.

3. Heat a small amount of water with the olive oil in a large saucepan. Add in the celery, bay leaf, onion and garlic and cook for 2-3 minutes.

4. Add the butternut squash and cook for 2-3 minutes, stirring throughout. Add the vegetable stock and bring to the boil. Leave to simmer for 10-12 minutes, stirring occasionally.

5. Add in the peppers, tomatoes, broccoli, carrots, courgettes and kidney beans. Simmer for a further 5-6 minutes, or until the squash is cooked and tender. Add in the arrowroot to thicken.

6. Remove from the heat and transfer the cooked vegetables to a baking dish.

Sweet Potato & Vegetable Shepherd's Pie cont/.

7. Take the sweet potato mash and add a little boiled water – mix well. Cover the vegetables with the mash, pressing down with a fork.

8. Place in the centre of the oven and cook for 15 minutes. Remove from the oven and serve into dishes.

Bengali-Style Potatoes & Spinach (Serves 6)

Ingredients

700g/1lb 8oz firm potatoes (cut into 1 inch/2 1/2cm chunks)
450g/1lb of spinach
150ml/2/3 cup of cold water
2 cloves of garlic (crushed)
1 onion (thinly sliced)
1 inch piece of fresh root ginger (finely chopped)
1 tsp chilli powder
1 tsp black mustard seeds
1 tsp salt
2 tbsps vegetable oil

Directions

1. Heat some water in a saucepan to boiling point and add the spinach. Cook for 2-3 minutes, drain thoroughly and set aside to cool. Once cooled, squeeze out any remaining juice with your hands, discarding the juice.

2. Heat the vegetable oil in a large saucepan and add the mustard seeds. Cook over a medium heat for a few minutes, until they start to spatter. Stir in the garlic, onion and ginger and cook for 4-5 minutes, stirring frequently.

3. Add the chilli powder, salt, potato chunks and cold water. Bring to the boil and cook for 8-10 minutes, stirring occasionally.

4. Add the drained spinach, cover and simmer for 12-15 minutes, until the potatoes are tender. Serve hot.

Boozy Sweet Potatoes! (Serves 4-8)

Ingredients

375g/2 1/2 cups of cooked, mashed sweet potatoes
75ml/1/3 cup Jack Daniels Whiskey
50g/1/2 cup of light brown sugar
3-4 tbsps butter
pecan halves (for topping)
salt (to season)

Boozy Sweet Potatoes! cont/.
Directions
1. Preheat the oven to 170C/325F/Gas mark 3. Grease a casserole dish.

2. Place the mashed potatoes, brown sugar, butter, whiskey and salt in a bowl and combine together well.

3. Transfer the mixture to the casserole dish and top with pecan halves. Place in the oven for 20-25 minutes.

4. Serve immediately.

Cajun Wedges (Serves 12)
Ingredients
12 medium sized baking potatoes (washed & cut into 1 1/2 cm wedges)
3 tbsps cajun seasoning
250g/2 1/2 cups of Cheddar cheese (finely grated)
10-12 spring onions (chopped)
6 tbsps olive oil

Directions
1. Preheat the oven to 225C/450F/Gas mark 7. Line 2 large baking trays with baking paper.

2. Place the oil and cajun seasoning in a jug and mix together.

3. Place the potato wedges inside a large, sealable plastic bag and pour in the seasoned oil (you may need to split the wedges and oil between 2 bags). Seal the bag and shake.

4. Turn the potatoes out onto the baking trays, spacing the wedges out evenly, not overlapping. Place in the oven and bake for 35-40 minutes, until cooked and golden brown.

5. Remove from the oven and transfer to a large serving dish. Sprinkle with cheese and chopped spring onions and serve hot.

Chard & Potato (Serves 2)

Ingredients

250g/9oz potatoes (peeled & cut into large chunks)
500g/1lb 1oz chard (large stalks removed & cut into 5cm ribbons)
2 cloves of garlic (finely chopped)
2 tbsps olive oil
salt & black peppers (to season)

Directions

1. Boil the potatoes for 8-10 minutes, until half cooked. Add the chard to the water with the potatoes and return to the boil. Cook for 3-4 minutes, until tender. Drain, reserving some of the liquid.

2. Heat the olive oil in a pan and add the garlic. Cook for 3-4 minutes. Add the chard and potatoes and season with salt and black pepper, according to taste.

3. Add a few tbsps of the reserved cooking liquid to the pan and crush a couple of the potato pieces, mixing them into the liquid. Cook for 3-4 minutes, until the liquid looks like a sauce. Serve as an accompaniment with red meat, chicken or fish.

Cheddar & Chive Mash (Serves 4)

Ingredients

225g/1 cup of mature Cheddar Cheese
225ml/1 cup of heated milk
2 tbsps butter
900g/2lb potatoes (peeled & cut into chunks)
1 tbsp chives (chopped)
1/2 tsp onion powder
salt & black pepper (to season)

Directions

1. Boil the potato chunks for 15-20 minutes, until tender. Drain well and return to the saucepan.

2. Remove from the heat and add the butter, milk, onion powder and mash well. Season with salt and black pepper and mash again.

Cheddar & Chive Mash cont/.

3. Gradually stir in the Cheddar cheese and return to a gentle heat. Mix continuously, until all of the cheese has melted.

4. Transfer the mash into a serving bowl and sprinkle over the top with the chopped chives. Serve immediately.

Chilli Roast Potatoes (Serves 6)

Ingredients

1kg/2lbs 4oz potatoes (peeled & cut into 2 inch chunks)
1/2 tsp chilli powder
2 tsps paprika powder
6 tbsps olive oil
1 1/2 tbsps sesame oil
1 tbsp fresh coriander (chopped)
salt & black pepper (to season)

Directions

1. Preheat the oven to 200C/400F/Gas mark 6.

2. Boil the potatoes for 5 minutes. Drain thoroughly, return to the saucepan and remove any excess water by shaking the pan over a low heat.

3. Place a lid over the saucepan and shake the potatoes well, to roughen the edges.

4. Heat the oil in a roasting tin and stir in the paprika and chilli powders. Add the potatoes and season with salt and black pepper, according to taste.

5. Place in the oven for 45-50 minutes, basting frequently with the hot oil.

6. Remove from the oven and transfer to a serving dish. Garnish with coriander and serve immediately.

Cheesy-Broccoli Baked Potatoes (Serves 4)

Ingredients

55ml/1/4 cup of semi-skimmed milk
150g/1 1/2 cups of grated Cheddar cheese
4 baking potatoes
6 broccoli stalks
1/4 tsp black pepper

Directions

1. Preheat the oven to 180C/350F/Gas mark 4.

2. Scrub the potatoes and pierce well several times. Bake for around 60 minutes (or until just cooked – this will depend on size).

3. Peel the broccoli stems and steam or boil in a pan until tender. Allow to cool for 1-2 minutes, chop finely and return to the pan.

4. Slice the baked potatoes in half and scoop out the potato into the pan with the broccoli. Add the milk, 3/4 of the cheese and black pepper. Mash together well.

5. Spoon the potato mixture back into the potato jackets and sprinkle with the remaining cheese. Return to the oven and bake for a further 10-15 minutes.

Chinese-Style Potatoes (Serves 4-6)

Ingredients

6 medium potatoes (scrubbed & cut into 1 inch/2.5 cm chunks)
600g/1 lb 5 oz canned, red kidney beans (drained & rinsed)
2 cloves of garlic (crushed)
1 large fresh chilli (seeded & sliced)
4 spring onions (sliced)
3 tbsps spy sauce
2 tbsps sunflower oil
1 1/2 tbsps sesame oil
1 tbsp sesame seeds
salt & black pepper (to season)
fresh parsley (chopped)

Chinese-Style Potatoes cont/.

Directions

1. Boil the potatoes for 10-12 minutes, until just tender. Drain and set aside.

2. Heat the sunflower oil in a large frying pan (or wok) and add the chilli and onion. Cook for 1-2 minutes. Add the garlic and fry for 30 seconds. Stir in the potatoes, coating them well.

3. Add the kidney beans, soy sauce and sesame oil and stir together well. Season with salt and black pepper, according to taste. Cook for 3-4 minutes, until all the vegetables are heated through.

4. Sprinkle with sesame seeds and garnish with chopped parsley.

5. Serve immediately.

Colcannon Mash (Serves 4-6)

Ingredients

900g/2lbs potatoes (peeled & cut into chunks)
1/2 savoy cabbage (finely shredded)
bunch of spring onions (finely chopped)
1-2 tsps butter
1-2 tbsps milk

Directions

1. Preheat the oven to 200C/400F/Gas mark 6.

2. Boil the potatoes for 12-15 minutes, until soft. For the last 7-9 minutes, add the shredded cabbage.

3. Drain thoroughly and add the butter and milk. Mash well and stir the chopped spring onions through the mash.

Duchesse Potatoes (Serves 4-6)

Ingredients

450g/1lb potatoes (peeled & thickly sliced)

1 large egg

1 large egg yolk

1 large egg & 1 tbsp milk (beaten – to glaze)

25g/1oz butter

olive oil

fresh nutmeg (grated)

salt & black pepper (to season)

Directions

1. Preheat the oven to 200C/400F/Gas mark 6.

2. Boil the potatoes for 10-12 minutes, until tender. Drain well and return to the pan. Shake the pan over the top of the still-hot hob for 1 minute, in order to dry the potatoes.

3. Press the potatoes through a ricer, or fine sieve; into a large bowl. Add the butter and mix together well with a wooden spoon, until smooth and creamy.

4. Mix the egg and egg yolk together and gradually beat them into the potato mixture. Add a little nutmeg and then season with salt and black pepper. Beat the mixture again, until light and fluffy.

5. Lightly grease a baking tray and carefully spoon the potato into an icing bag with a 1/2 inch star-shaped nozzle. Pipe the potato onto the baking tray, in mini-rounds with peaked tops.

6. Brush the tops with the egg/milk glaze and place in the oven for 20-25 minutes, until golden brown.

7. Serve immediately

Garlic & Herb Cheese Mash (Serves 4)

Ingredients

75g/1/3 cup of soft cheese, with garlic & herbs
55ml/1/4 cup of milk (heated to warm)
900g/2lbs potatoes (peeled & cut into 2 inch chunks)
salt & black pepper (to season)

Directions

1. Place the potato chunks into a saucepan, cover with cold water and bring to the boil. Reduce the heat and simmer for about 20 minutes, until tender.

2. Drain the potatoes through a colander and return them to the saucepan. Cook for 20-30 seconds more, to expel any residual water.

3. Mash the potatoes in the pan until they are well mashed and have no lumps. Add the soft cheese and beat, combining the mixture well. Pour in the heated milk, little by little, mixing continuously.

4. Season with salt and black pepper, according to taste and transfer to a serving dish. Serve immediately.

Greek-Style Lemon Potatoes (Serves 4-6)

Ingredients

950g/2lbs potatoes (peeled & cut into thick slices)
juice & grated zest of 1 lemon
55g/2oz butter
salt & black pepper (to season)
lemon slices, twisted (to garnish)

Directions

1. Preheat the oven to 200C/400F/Gas mark 6.

2. Layer the potato slices inside a gratin dish and sprinkle over the grated lemon zest and half of the lemon juice. Season with salt and black pepper, according to taste.

3. Dot the butter evenly over the top of the potatoes and place in the oven for 12-15 minutes.

4. Remove from the oven and drain off any excess fat from the dish. Evenly pour the remaining lemon juice over the potatoes and gently toss together. Return to the oven and bake for a further 20 minutes, until tender and golden.

5. Transfer to a serving dish and garnish with lemon slices. Serve hot.

Homemade Roasted Chunky Chips (Serves 4)

Ingredients
900g/2lbs red potatoes (scrubbed & thoroughly dried)
1 tbsp olive oil
Salt

Directions
1. Preheat the oven to 230C/450F/Gas mark 8.

2. Slice the potatoes in half, lengthways and then slice them lengthways again, into 1 inch thick wedges. Dry with a cloth and transfer them to a bowl.

3. Add the olive oil to the bowl and season with salt. Toss together well, to ensure an even coating of oil. Transfer to a baking tray and place in the oven for 30-35 minutes, until crispy and golden.

4. Serve immediately.

Indonesian-Style Potatoes
Ingredients
500g/1lb 2oz potatoes (peeled & diced)
1-2 spring onions (chopped)
2 celery stalks (chopped)
1 shallot (chopped & fried)
1 egg (whole)
1 egg yolk
3 tbsps vegetable oil
salt & black pepper (to season)
oil (for deep fat frying)

Directions
1. Heat the vegetable oil in a large saucepan and add the potatoes. Fry for 5-8 minutes, until tender. Set aside for 5 minutes and then remove the potatoes with a slotted spoon.

2. Place the potatoes in a food processor and add the spring onions, fried shallot and celery. Season with salt and black pepper, according to taste. Blend until well mixed. Add the egg and blend the mixture again.

3. Using your hands, shape the mixture into 1 1/2" sized balls and then flatten them a little, gently, with your palm. Place on a plate, cover and refrigerate for 1 hour.

4. Heat the oil for frying.

5. Place the egg yolk in a bowl and beat together. Dip each of the potato 'cakes' in the egg yolk. Carefully drop them into the hot oil and fry for a few minutes, until golden and crisp. Remove with a slotted spoon and serve.

Lyonnaise Potatoes (Serves 4-6)
Ingredients
900g/2lbs potatoes (scrubbed)
2 onions (cut into thin rings)
1 tbsp fresh parsley (chopped)
4 tbsps olive oil
salt & black pepper (to season)

Directions

1. Boil the potatoes, (with their skins), for 15 minutes. Drain and allow to cool a little. Cut into evenly sized slices, about 1cm thick.

2. Heat the olive oil in a large frying pan and add the onions. Cook for 4-5 minutes, until tender and golden. Remove the onions with a slotted spoon and keep warm.

3. Add the potato slices to the frying pan and season with a little salt. Cook for 3-4 minutes on each side, until golden brown. Return the onions to the frying pan. Season with salt and black pepper, according to taste and cook for a further couple of minutes.

4. Transfer the potatoes to a serving dish and garnish with freshly chopped parsley.

Mashed Potato Mediterranean-Style (Serves 4)

Ingredients

775g/1lb 11oz potatoes (peeled & cut into chunks)
1 red pepper
1 yellow pepper
10-12 black pitted olives
180ml/3/4 cup milk
olive oil
salt & black pepper (to season)

Directions

1. Boil the potatoes for 18-20 minutes, until tender. Whilst the potatoes are cooking, grill the peppers until slightly blackened. Remove from the grill and cover. Once cooled a little, slice the peppers and keep warm.

2. Drain the potatoes and return to the saucepan. Add the milk and heat until the milk is almost to the boil. Remove from the heat.

3. Mash the potatoes with the milk, until smooth and fluffy. Transfer to a serving bowl and top with the pepper slices and black olives. Drizzle over a little olive oil and serve immediately.

Mini Potato Soufflés (Serves 8-12)

Ingredients

1 1/2kg/8 1/2 cups of potatoes (cut into 1/4 cm slices)
2 tsps salt
vegetable oil (for deep frying)

Directions

1. Place the potato slices in a large bowl of water and leave for 30-40 minutes. Drain and dry the slices.

2. Fill two large saucepans with vegetable oil, to about 1/3 full. Heat the oil in one of the saucepans to 170C/325F (using a deep-fat dryer thermometer). Heat the oil in the other pan to 190C/375F.

3. Drop the potato sliced into the first saucepan and fry for 4 minutes. Remove with a slotted spoon and drop into the other saucepan, frying for 2-3 minutes, until the potatoes 'puff up'.

4. Remove the soufflés with a slotted spoon and drain on paper kitchen towel. Transfer to a large serving dish and sprinkle with salt.

5. Serve immediately.

Minted New Potatoes with Petit Pois (Serves 4-6)

Ingredients

900g/2lbs New potatoes (scrubbed & thickly sliced)
180g/1 1/4 cups frozen petit pois
2 tbsps fresh mint (chopped)
3 tbsps olive oil
salt & black pepper (to season)

Directions

1. Heat the olive oil in a large frying pan and add the potatoes. Cook for 2-3 minutes, each side, until golden. NB. You may need to do this in 2-3 batches, in order to brown the potatoes.

2. Return all of the potatoes to the frying pan and cover them loosely. Cook for a further 12-15 minutes.

3. Towards the end of the potato cooking time, cook the petit pois for 2-3 minutes. Drain and add to the frying pan with the potatoes. Cook for 2-3 minutes more.

4. Remove from the heat and add the chopped mint. Season with salt and black pepper, according to taste and serve.

Mixed Roast Potatoes & Vegetables

Ingredients

1kg/2 1/2lb mixed root vegetables, such as sweet potatoes, carrots, swede, parsnips, potatoes (peeled & cut into large chunks)
200g/7oz whole shallots (peeled)
3 sprigs of fresh thyme
3 sprigs of fresh rosemary
2 tbsps olive oil
1 tsp rock salt
1 tsp fresh black peppercorns

Directions

1. Preheat the oven to 220C/425F/Gas mark 7.

2. Place all the vegetables in a saucepan and cover with boiling water. Bring to the boil, reduce the heat and simmer for 6-7 minutes.

3. Drain the vegetables and place in an appropriately sized roasting tin. Brush the vegetables with the oil and sprinkle over with salt and black peppercorns.

4. Evenly place the herb sprigs in the roasting tin and place in the centre of the oven. Roast for 35-40 minutes, turning halfway through cooking.

5. Remove from the oven when golden brown and crisp. Serve immediately.

Oat-Fried Potatoes (Serves 8)

Ingredients

900g/2lbs small new potatoes
2 large eggs (beaten)
6 tbsps oats
50g/1/4 cup butter

Directions

1. Boil the potatoes for 12-15 minutes, until just tender. Drain well and set aside to cool.

2. Place the eggs in a shallow dish and dip in the potatoes. Place the oats on a plate and coat each of the potatoes, pressing them firmly with your fingers so that the oats stick.

3. Melt the butter in a frying pan and add the coated potatoes. Cook for 5-6 minutes, turning them frequently, until golden brown.

4. Serve hot.

Oven-Roasted Red Potatoes with Red Onion (Serves 4)

Ingredients

1kg/2.2lbs red potatoes (scrubbed & cut into 3/4 inch chunks)
2 red onions (sliced)
2-3 tbsps olive oil
1 1/2 tbsp red wine vinegar
salt & black pepper (to season)

Directions

1. Preheat the oven to 220F/425F/Gas mark 7. Pour the olive oil into a roasting tin and place in the oven to heat up for 6-8 minutes.

2. Remove tin from the oven and carefully add the potatoes and onion, turning them to ensure a good covering of oil. Sprinkle evenly over the top with the red wine vinegar and season with salt and black pepper, according to taste.

3. Return to the oven and cook for 40-45 minutes, until the potatoes are crisp. Serve immediately.

Pesto & Parmesan New Potatoes (Serves 6)

Ingredients

750g/1lb 10oz new potatoes (scrubbed & halved)
40g/1.5oz parmesan cheese (coarsely grated)
4-5 tsps pesto
salt & black pepper

Directions

1. Boil the potatoes for 12-15 minutes, until tender. Drain and set aside to cool a little.

2. Add the pesto to the potatoes and toss gently. Season with a little salt and black pepper and sprinkle over the top with the parmesan cheese.

3. Serve immediately.

Pommes Anna (Serves 6)

Ingredients

1kg/2.2lbs floury potatoes (peeled & thinly sliced)
3 cloves of garlic (crushed)
140g/2/3 cup butter (melted)
salt & black pepper (to season)
butter (to grease)

Directions

1. Preheat the oven to 200C/400F/Gas mark 6.

2. Grease a large ovenproof dish with butter and layer the base with overlapping slices of potato. Sprinkle over a little of the garlic and pour over some of the butter. Season with salt and black pepper.

3. Continue this process of layering and flavouring the potatoes until all of the potato slices have been used.

4. Cover with foil and place in the oven for 40-45 minutes. Serve hot.

Potatoes Dauphinois (Serves 4)

Ingredients

170ml/3/4 cup of double cream
150ml/2/3 cup of milk
10g/1/2oz butter
700g/1lb 8oz potatoes (thinly sliced)
75g/3/4 cup of mature English Cheddar cheese (grated)
1 clove of garlic (crushed)
ground nutmeg
salt & black pepper (to season)

Directions

1. Preheat the oven to 170C/325F/Gas mark 3 and grease a 1.1 litre ovenproof dish.

2. Place the grated cheese and crushed garlic in a small bowl and add a little nutmeg. Combine well.

3. Place a layer of potato slices in the base of the dish. Season with a little salt and black pepper and sprinkle over some of the cheese/garlic mixture.

4. Repeat this process, finishing with a layer of potato.

5. Pour the cream and milk into a large mixing jug and mix together well. Pour over the potatoes and dot the top evenly with butter.

6. Place in the oven for 1 1/2 - 1 3/4 hours. Remove from the oven and serve hot. Brown the top lightly under the grill before serving, if desired.

Potato Gratin (Serves 4-6)

Ingredients - Potatoes

4-5 large potatoes (cut into 1/4 inch thick slices)
450ml/2 cups double cream
3 large eggs (beaten)
55g/2oz Gruyere cheese (grated)
55g/2oz Parmesan cheese (grated)
1/4 tsp fresh grated nutmeg
salt & black pepper (to season)

Ingredients - Topping

55g/2oz Gruyere cheese
30g/1 1/4oz butter (cubed)

Directions

1. Preheat the oven to 150C/300F/Gas mark 2-3. Grease a 11 x 8 inch gratin dish.

2. Place the double cream and eggs in a large bowl and beat together well. Add the Parmesan and Gruyere cheese and beat again. Mix in the grated nutmeg, followed by salt and black pepper.

3. Add the potato slices to the cream/eggs mixture and toss well, until well covered. Pour into the gratin dish and sprinkle with the Gruyere cheese topping and dot with the cubed butter pieces.

4. Place in the oven and cook for 1 1/4 to 1 1/2 hours, until tender and golden. Serve piping hot.

Potato Kebabs (Serves 8)

Ingredients - Kebabs

26-32 baby new potatoes
250g/9oz bacon (cut into strips)
2 onions (cut into quarters)
2 red peppers (cut into large chunks)
1 pineapple (cut into triangles)

Ingredients -Basting

1 1/2 tbsps olive oil
2 tsps honey
2 tbsps red wine vinegar

Directions

1. Boil the potatoes for 10-12 minutes, until just tender.

2. Thread the potatoes and other ingredients onto skewers, alternating each ingredient.

3. Place the olive oil, red wine vinegar and honey in a bowl and mix together. Brush the vegetables, coating them all evenly.

4. Preheat the grill to a medium heat and grill for 10-12 minutes, basting and turning them regularly. Serve hot.

Potato Latkes (Makes 12)

Ingredients

500g/1lb 2oz potatoes (peeled & coarsely grated)
1/2 tbsp onion (grated)
20g/3/4oz self-raising flour
1 egg
1/4 tsp fresh nutmeg (grated)
salt & black pepper (to season)
vegetable oil (for shallow frying)

Directions

1. Soak the grated potato in water for 1 hour. Drain thoroughly and pat dry with paper kitchen towel. Place the egg, flour, nutmeg and onion in a bowl and beat together. Stir in the potato and season with salt and black pepper, according to taste.

2. Heat about 1cm deep vegetable oil in a frying pan and carefully drop in 1 tbsp of the potato mixture. Cook for 3-4 minutes each side, until golden brown. Remove with a slotted spoon and drain on paper kitchen towel. Keep warm and cook the remaining mixture. Best served hot.

Roasted Vegetables (Serves 4)

Ingredients

4 medium potatoes (peeled & halved)
4 brown onions (peeled)
4 pieces of pumpkin, same size as potato halves (peeled)
1 tbsp olive oil

Directions

1. Preheat the oven to 180C/350F/Gas mark 4. Boil the potatoes for 5-6 minutes. Drain well and return to the pan and dry on paper kitchen towel. Return to the pan and shake with the lid on to roughen up the edges a little. Set aside for a few minutes to cool.

2. Place the pumpkin, onions and potatoes in a baking tray and brush with olive oil. Place in the oven for 55-60 minutes, until golden brown and crisp. Transfer to a serving dish and serve immediately.

Saute Potatoes (Serves 4)
Ingredients
700g/1lb 8oz medium potatoes (scrubbed)
2 tbsps vegetable oil
30g/1 1/4oz butter
2 tbsps fresh parsley (chopped)
salt & black pepper (to season)

Directions
1. Boil the potatoes for 8-10 minutes, until almost tender. Drain and return to the pan, cover to keep them warm.

2. Once cool enough to hold, peel the potatoes and cut them into wedges.

3. Heat the oil in a frying pan and add the butter, melt until just bubbling and carefully add the potatoes.

4. Cook over a medium heat for 4-5 minutes, until golden brown. Season with salt and black pepper, according to taste.

Soured Cream Jackets (Serves 8)
Ingredients
620ml/2 3/4 cups of soured cream
8 large jacket potatoes (pricked & brushed with oil)
1 tsp chilli powder
1 1/2 tbsps dill (chopped)
5 tbsps chives (chopped)
2 tbsps capers (chopped)
black pepper (to season)

Directions
1. Preheat the oven to 200C/400F/Gas mark 6. Place the soured cream, chives, dill, capers and chilli powder in a bowl and mix together. Season with black pepper, according to taste. Cover and refrigerate.

2. Place the potatoes in the oven for 1 to 1 1/4 hours, or until cooked. Remove from the oven, split and fill with the chilled soured cream. Serve.

Spicy Baked Potatoes (Serves 4)

Ingredients

4 baking potatoes (scrubbed & pricked with a fork)

425g/1 3/4 cups canned chickpeas (drained)

150ml/2/3 cup natural yoghurt (unsweetened)

1 tbsp vegetable oil

1 tsp ground coriander

1 tsp ground cumin

3 tbsps fresh coriander leaves (chopped)

salt & black pepper (to season)

Directions

1. Preheat the oven to 200C/400F/Gas mark 6. Bake the potatoes in the oven for 1 1/4-1 1/2 hours, until soft. Leave to cool for 10 minutes.

2. Whilst the potatoes are cooling, place the chickpeas in a bowl and mash with a potato masher or fork. Add the ground coriander and cumin, followed by half of the chopped coriander leaves. Cover and set aside.

3. Halve the cooked potatoes and scoop out the flesh into a bowl, retaining the skins. Mash the potato in the bowl and gradually mix in the chickpea mixture, followed by the yoghurt. Season with salt and black pepper, according to taste.

4. Fill the potato jackets with the mixture and place on a baking tray. Return to the oven and cook for 12-15 minutes, until heated through.

5. Remove from the oven and sprinkle with the remaining chopped coriander leaves. Serve immediately.

Quick n Easy Bombay Potatoes (Serves 4)

Ingredients

1kg/2.2lbs potatoes (peeled & cut into 1/2 inch pieces)
2 onions (chopped)
2 cloves of garlic
1 1/2 tbsps olive oil
2 tsps ground cumin
2 tsps ground coriander
4 tsps curry powder
salt & black pepper (to season)

Directions

1. Boil the potatoes for 12-15 minutes, until just tender. Drain well (reserving the liquid) and return to the pan.

2. Whilst the potatoes are cooking, heat the olive oil in a large frying pan and add the onion. Cook for 5-6 minutes, until just tender. Add the spices and garlic and cook for a further 2 minutes.

3. Add the cooked potatoes to the frying pan and gently stir in. Add 1-2 tbsps of the reserved liquid, to loosen the mixture a little. Cook for 3-5 minutes. Season with salt and black pepper, according to taste.

4. Transfer to a serving dish and garnish with parsley. Best served piping hot.

Spinach & Potato Croquettes (Serves 4)

Ingredients

450g/1lb potatoes (peeled & cut into large chunks)
450g/1lb spinach (washed & stalks removed)
2 tbsps mature Cheddar cheese (grated)
80g dried white breadcrumbs
2 eggs (lightly beaten)
1 egg yolk (lightly beaten)
3 tbsps plain flour
salt & black pepper (to season)
vegetable oil (for deep-frying)

Directions

1. Boil the potatoes for 12-15 minutes, until tender. Drain thoroughly and then push through a sieve, into a large bowl.

2. Place the spinach in a large saucepan. Cover and cook (stirring occasionally) over a gentle heat for 5-6 minutes, until tender. Drain thoroughly and then chop the spinach finely.

3. Add the spinach to the bowl holding the potato and mix together. Beat in the egg yolk, followed by the grated cheese. Season with salt and black pepper, according to taste. Combine all of the ingredients well.

4. Turn out the mixture onto a floured work surface and roll into a thick sausage shape, about 2 inches long.

5. Place the flour on a plate and season with salt and black pepper. Place the breadcrumbs on a separate plate. Place the beaten eggs in a shallow bowl.

6. Roll each of the croquettes in the flour, followed by the egg and then through the breadcrumbs, coating each evenly.

7. Heat enough vegetable oil for deep frying to about 180C/350F. Carefully drop in each croquette and fry for 2-3 minutes each, until golden brown. Remove with a slotted spoon and drain off any excess fat on paper kitchen towel. Serve hot.

Sweet Potato & Beetroot in Honey (Serves 4)

Ingredients

2 large raw beetroots (peeled & cut into 1cm/1/2 inch strips)
2 small sweet potatoes (peeled & cut into 1cm/1/2 inch strips)
1 1/2 tbsps honey
4 tsps Grand Marnier
3 tbsps orange juice
1 1/2 tsps orange peel (grated)
35g/1 1/4oz butter

Directions

1. Boil the sweet potato and beetroot for 10-15 minutes, until just tender (in separate saucepans).

2. Heat the butter in a frying pan and stir in the Grand Marnier, orange peel, orange juice and honey. Cook for 2-3 minutes, until all of the ingredients are well combined and the honey has melted.

3. Add the beetroot and sweet potato and cook for 3-4 minutes, until heated through.

4. Serve immediately.

Cheese & Potato Scones (Makes 16-20)

Ingredients

200g/7oz potatoes (cooked, mashed & cooled)
200g/1 3/4 cups mature Cheddar cheese (grated)
200g/1 1/3 cups self-raising flour
2 eggs
2 tbsps milk
3 tsps baking powder
1/2 tsp salt
1/4 tsp mustard powder
30g/1 1/4 oz butter (chopped)
vegetable oil (for greasing)

Directions

1. Preheat the oven to 190C/375F/Gas mark 5. Lightly grease 2 baking trays.

2. Sift the flour, salt, mustard and baking powder into a large bowl and mix together. Rub the butter into the mixture by hand, until it becomes breadcrumb-like.

3. Stir in the cheese, mixing it in well. Push the cold mashed potato through a sieve into the bowl and combine, using a blunt knife.

4. Place the eggs and milk in a mixing jug and beat together. Gradually pour into the potato mixture, combing well – only pour enough in to make a soft dough.

5. Flour a clean surface and turn the dough out onto the top. Knead the dough lightly and roll out into a 3/4 inch thickness. Using a scone cutter, cut out the desired amount of rounds and place on the baking trays.

6. Place in the oven for 12-15 minutes, until golden brown. Remove from the oven and transfer to a wire cooling rack. Best served warm.

Orange & Dark Chocolate Potato Cake (Serves 4-6)

Ingredients

130g/1 cup potatoes (boiled, mashed & cooled)
240g/2 cups self raising flour
230g/1 cup demerara sugar
120g/4 1/2 oz dark chocolate
180g/3/4 cup butter
3 large eggs (beaten)
35g/1/4 cup cocoa powder
Juice & grated rind of 1 large orange

Directions

1. Preheat the oven to 180C/350F/Gas mark 4. Grease a 24cm cake tin with butter.

2. Place the mashed potato, sugar and butter in a large bowl and beat together, until smooth and light.

3. Place the chocolate in a bowl and place over a pan of simmering water. Stir until melted.

4. Beat the eggs into the mashed potato mixture and then gradually mix in the melted chocolate.

5. Stir in the orange juice and grated rind, followed by carefully folding in the cocoa powder.

6. Transfer the mixture into the cake tin and place in the oven for 35-40 minutes, until firm to the touch and golden.

Nut & Potato Cookies (Makes 12)

Ingredients

90g/2/3 cup sweet potatoes (cooked & mashed until smooth)
65g/1/2 cup self raising flour
40g/1/4 cup butter (softened)
30g/1.2oz pecans (chopped)
1 small egg
juice & grated rind of 1/2 large orange
65g/1/4 cup light brown sugar
1/4 tsp vanilla essence
1/4 tsp grated nutmeg
pinch of salt

Directions

1. Preheat the oven to 200C/400F/Gas mark 6. Grease 1-2 baking trays with butter.

2. Place the cream, butter and sugar in a large bowl and beat together until fluffy, using a wooden spoon. Gradually beat in the egg.

3. Add the potato, orange juice and rind and vanilla. Combine well.

4. Sift the flour, nutmeg and salt into the mixture and combine together well. Stir in the chopped pecans.

5. Carefully drops teaspoons of the batter onto the baking tray, making sure that they are spaced well apart – as they will spread out during baking.

6. Place in the oven for 12-15 minutes, until golden brown. Remove from the oven and place the cookies on a wire cooling rack.

Potato, Oat & Apple Muffins (Makes 24)

Ingredients

400g/2 2/3 cups sweet potatoes (cooked & mashed)
150g/2 cups rolled oats
200g/1 1/2 cups wholewheat flour
300g/1 1/2 cups sugar
2 apples (peeled & finely chopped)
360ml/1 1/2 cups plain yoghurt
2 eggs
4 egg whites
4 tbsps vegetable oil
3 tsps ground cinnamon
1 tsp baking powder
1 tsp baking soda
1/4 tsp salt

Directions

1. Preheat the oven to 180C/350F/Gas mark 4. Grease 2 x 12 muffin baking tins.

3. Place the flour, sugar, rolled oats, baking powder, baking soda, salt, cinnamon and chopped apples in a large bowl and combine well.

4. Add the eggs, egg whites, mashed potatoes, yoghurt and vegetable oil and mix well.

5. Spoon the mixture evenly into the muffin tins, filling each to 3/4 full. Place in the oven and bake for 20-25 minutes, until firm to the touch and golden.

6. Remove from the oven and place on a wire cooling rack to cool.

Praline & Sweet Potato Pie (Serves 8)

Ingredients - Pie

2 medium sweet potatoes

2 large eggs

1 x 9 inch ready-made pie crust (uncooked)

200g/1 cup of light brown sugar

60g/1/4 cup of butter (softened)

110ml/1/2 cup of evaporated milk

1/2 tsp ground ginger

1/2 tsp grated nutmeg

1/2 tsp ground cinnamon

1/4 tsp salt

Ingredients - Praline

1/4 cup of pecans (chopped)

1 tbsp butter

2 tbsps light brown sugar

Ingredients - Topping

1/2 cup of pecans (halved)

1 tbsp light brown sugar

1 tbsp butter

Directions - Pie

1. Gently boil the potatoes for 35-40 minutes, until tender. Drain and leave to cool a little.

2. Once cooled enough to touch, peel the potatoes and place them in a large bowl. Mash the potatoes, but not so being completely smooth.

3. Add the butter, evaporated milk, eggs, brown sugar, salt, cinnamon, nutmeg and ginger and mash together well. Set aside.

4. Preheat the oven to 200C/400F/Gas mark 4.

Praline & Sweet Potato Pie cont/.

Directions - Praline

1. Melt the butter in a saucepan and add the sugar. Gently heat for a couple of minutes, until the mixture is smooth. Stir in the pecan pieces, combining them well.

2. Remove from the heat and spread the mixture over the base of the pie crust.

3. Spoon the sweet potato mixture over the top, spreading it out evenly. Place the pie on a baking tray and bake in the oven for 10 minutes.

4. Reduce the temperature to 180C/350F/Gas mark 4 and continue to bake for 40-45 minutes, until cooked and set.

5. Remove from the oven and place on a wire cooling rack to cool.

Directions - Topping

1. Melt the butter in a saucepan and add one tbsp of brown sugar. Gently heat for a couple of minutes, stirring frequently, until the mixture is smooth.

2. Stir in the pecan halves and cook, stirring frequently, for 2-3 minutes until toasted. Remove from the heat and leave to cool a little for a few minutes.

3. Top the pie with the mixture, spreading it evenly.

INDEX

B - H   92

I - P   93

P - Z   94

Conversions   95

B

Baked Jackets with Smoked Haddock pp.31
Bengali-Style Potatoes & Spinach pp.61
Bolton Hot-Pot pp.41
Boozy Sweet Potatoes pp.61
Bubble and Squeak pp.42

C

Cabbage & Potato Cakes with Poached Eggs pp.32
Cajun Wedges pp.62
Carrot & Potato Souffle pp.43
Chard & Potato pp.63
Cheddar & Chive Mash pp.63
Cheese & Potato Casserole with Sour Cream pp.44
Cheese & Potato Scones pp.85
Cheesy Broccoli Baked Potatoes pp.65
Chilled Potato Soup pp.13
Chilli Roast Potatoes pp.64
Chinese-Style Potatoes pp.65
Classic American Potato Salad pp.23
Colcannon Mash pp.66
Corned Beef & Potato Hash pp.44
Cream of Potato Soup pp.14
Creamy Chicken Jackets pp.33
Creamy Potato & Pepper Salad pp.23
Crispy Potato Skin & Tex Mex Dips pp.14

D

Dry Potato Curry pp.45
Duchesses Potatoes pp.67

E

Egg & Potato Mayonnaise pp.24

F

Fish & Potato Cakes with Hot Sauce pp.34

G

Garlic & Herb Cheese Mash pp.68
Greek-Style Lemon Potatoes pp.68

H

Hash Browns pp.7
Herbed Potato Cake pp.46
Homemade Roasted Chunky Chips pp.69
Hot Beef & Potato Supper pp.47
Hot-Pot-Lamb-Chops pp.48

I

Indonesian-Style Potatoes pp.70

L

Leek & Cheddar Stuffed PotatoJacket pp.35
Leek & Sweet Potato Cakes pp.36
Lemon Chicken & Potato Wedge Bake pp.49
Lyonnaise Potatoes pp.70

M

Mashed Potato Mediterranean-Style pp.71
Mediterranean-Style Potato Salad pp.25
Mexican Potatoes pp.8
Mexican-Style Chicken & Potatoes pp.50
Mini Potato Souffles pp.72
Minted New Potatoes with Petit Pois pp.72
Mixed Roast Potatoes & Vegetables pp.73
Moroccan-Style Potato & Chickpea Soup pp.15

N

New Potato & Shallot Salad pp.26
Nut & Potato Cookies pp.87

O

Oat-Fried Potatoes pp.74
Olive & Caper Potato Cakes pp.16
Orange & Dark Chocolate Potato Cake pp.86
Oven-Roasted Red Potatoes with Red Onion pp.74

P

Pesto & Parmesan New Potatoes pp.75
Pommes Anna pp.75
Potato & Aduki Bean Pie pp.51
Potato & Asparagus Quiche pp.37
Potato & Beetroot Flan pp.52
Potato & Chees Bake pp.53
Potato & Pasta Soup pp.17
Potato & Prawn Salad pp.29
Potato & Smoked Fish Chowder pp.18
Potato & Vegetable Patties pp.38
Potato & Vegetable Pizza pp.54
Potato Gratin pp.77
Potato Kebabs pp.78

P

Potato Latkes pp.79
Potato Pancake pp.10
Potato Scones pp.11
Potato, Bacon & Tomato Salad pp.27
Potato, Cheese & Bacon Omelette pp.8
Potato, Chorizo & Egg Brunch pp.9
Potato, Fennel & Carrot Salad pp.28
Potato, Oat & Apple Muffins pp.88
Potatoes Dauphinois pp.76
Praline & Sweet Potato Pie pp.89
Prawn & Potato Curry pp.55

Q

Quick & Easy Bombay Potatoes pp.82

R

Roasted Vegetables pp.79

S

Salad Nicoise pp.28
Sausage Hash pp.12
Saute Potatoes pp.80
Slow-Cook Thai Pumpkin & Sweet Potato Curry pp.56
Soured Cream Jackets pp.80
Spiced Sweet Potato Soup pp.20
Spicy Baked Potatoes pp.81
Spicy Pan Fried Potatoes & Beef pp.57
Spicy Potato & Chickpea Bites pp.19
Spicy Potato & Tomota Chowder pp.21
Spinach & Potato Croquettes pp.83
Spinach & Potato Patties pp.38
Sweet Potato & Beetroot in Honey pp.84
Sweet Potato & Chickpea Stew pp.58
Sweet Potato & Red Pepper Soup pp.22
Sweet Potato & Vegetable Shepherd's Pie pp.59

V

Veggie Filled Jacket Potatoes pp.39

W

Walnut & Potato Salad pp.30

Z

Zesty Tuna Jackets pp.40

Spoons to millilitres

1/2 Teaspoon	2.5ml	1 Tablespoon	15ml
1 Teaspoon	5ml	2 Tablespoons	30ml
1-1/2 Teaspoons	7.5ml	3 Tablespoon	45ml
2 Teaspoons	10 ml	4 Tablespoons	60ml

Grams to Ounces

10g	0.25oz	225g	8oz
15g	0.38oz	250g	9oz
25g	1oz	275g	10oz
50g	2oz	300g	11oz
75g	3oz	350g	12oz
110g	4oz	375g	13oz
150g	5oz	400g	14oz
175g	6oz	425g	15oz
200g	7oz	450g	16oz

Metric to Cups

Flour etc	115g	1 cup
Clear Honey etc	350g	1 cup
Liquids	225ml	1 cup

Liquid measures

5fl oz	1/4 pint	150ml
7.5fl oz		215ml
10fl oz	1/2 pint	275ml
15fl oz		425ml
20fl oz	1 pint	570ml
35fl oz	1-3/4 pints	1 litre

Temperature

Celsius	Farenheit	Gas Mark	Description
110c	225F	1/4	very cool
130c	250F	1/2	very cool
140c	275F	1	cool
150c	300F	2	cool
170c	325F	3	very moderate
180c	350F	4	moderate
190c	375F	5	moderate
200c	400F	6	moderately hot
220c	425F	7	hot
230c	450F	8	hot
240c	475F	9	very hot